Parenting Preschoolers with a Purpose

CARING FOR YOUR KIDS & YOURSELF

JOLENE L. ROEHLKEPARTAIN

Parenting Preschoolers with a Purpose
Caring for Your Kids and Yourself

By Jolene L. Roehlkepartain

Search Institute® and Developmental Assets® are trademarks of Search Institute.

Copyright © 2006 by Search Institute

A Search Institute Publication

10 9 8 7 6 5 4 3 2 1
Printed on acid-free paper in the United States of America.

Search Institute
615 First Avenue Northeast, Suite 125
Minneapolis, MN 55413
www.search-institute.org
612-376-8955 • 800-888-7828

ISBN-13: 978-1-57482-239-7
ISBN-10: 1-57482-239-X

CREDITS
EDITOR: Tenessa Gemelke
BOOK DESIGN: Cathy Spengler
PRODUCTION COORDINATOR: Mary Ellen Buscher

LIBRARY OF CONGRESS CATALOGING-IN-PUBLICATION DATA

Roehlkepartain, Jolene L., 1962-
  Parenting preschoolers with a purpose : the go-to guide to caring for your kids and yourself / Jolene L. Roehlkepartain.
     p. cm.
  Includes index.
  ISBN-13: 978-1-57482-239-7 (pbk. : alk. paper)
  ISBN-10: 1-57482-239-X (pbk. : alk. paper)
  1. Preschool children.
  2. Parenting.
  3. Child development.
  4. Child rearing.
  I. Search Institute (Minneapolis, Minn.)
  II. Title.

HQ774.5.R64 2006
649'.123--dc22

                              2006007040

To Julie Scroggins, Lori Katz, and Kim
and Quillan Roe—all who were instrumental
in giving my children a great start.

CONTENTS

INTRODUCTION

How You Parent Makes a Difference

When my first child became a preschooler, I was stumped. All the strategies I had used as a parent no longer worked.

I had always believed that parenting became easier as children grew older and more independent. I had survived the sleep-deprived stage of parenting an infant. I had succeeded in parenting a toddler. I was convinced that parenting a preschooler would be a snap.

Was I ever wrong.

Preschoolers are delightful people, but they can be hard on their parents. They're older and more clever, and they can create havoc for much longer periods of time. People had warned me about the terrible twos, but few had talked about the turbulent threes, the frustrating fours, and the finicky fives.

Although I loved and enjoyed my children a lot, I often felt puzzled by their behavior. When one of my preschoolers started kicking all the time (after never doing this as a toddler) and the other started scrambling behind the piano during meals, I knew I was in over my head.

Many adults enjoy the wonder of preschoolers. Three- to five-year-olds make insightful comments.

They're exuberant when they discover something new. They're energetic. Their giggles are infectious. They embrace life head-on. As an adult, I find children ages 3 to 5 to be one of my favorite age groups. But as a *parent,* I've found preschoolers to be one of the hardest age groups to manage.

Preschoolers go through difficult and demanding phases that frustrate and baffle parents. You're shocked when they swear. You feel flattened the first time they scream, "I hate you!" You're dumbfounded when your child refuses to eat or go to bed. The parenting techniques that once worked for you no longer have any effect on your child. Even after years of successfully managing your little one, you can't help but wonder what you've done wrong.

A Hopeful New Strategy

As I struggled with the ups and downs of raising preschoolers, I started reading parenting books and parenting magazines. I learned new tactics and ideas for dealing with every foreseeable challenge. At first this helped, but gradually I realized that something major was missing. After a while, I became weary of racing to the library every time one of my preschoolers did something I didn't understand. I needed something that would help me parent my children well—with a purpose. I wanted a framework that guided me as a parent, not just quick fixes to specific problems.

Then I discovered Search Institute's framework of Developmental Assets, and the pieces came together for me as a parent. The positive approach helped me make choices and stay focused on what is most important. The assets gave me the courage, confidence, perspective, and strategies I needed.

Yes, my preschool-age children still had meltdowns. Yes, I still had days when I questioned why I had even become a parent. But using the Developmental Assets framework as my compass gave me concrete direction and hope for success.

Why Developmental Assets Make a Difference

Search Institute, a nonprofit organization that works to promote healthy children, youth, and communities, has conducted extensive research in positive youth development. Researchers have reviewed more than 1,200 scientific studies to identify what children and teenagers need to thrive. Their work resulted in the Developmental Assets framework, a powerful context for thinking about the important things that help kids grow up and succeed. (See the complete list on pages 7–11.)

What are Developmental Assets? They're specific building blocks for raising healthy children. When preschoolers build these Developmental Assets with the help of parents and other caring adults, they're more likely to grow up responsible and successful. Search Institute research consistently shows that having more of these Developmental Assets makes a major difference in the lives of young people. For example, researchers have found that children and teenagers who have more assets in their lives are:

- more likely to behave in positive ways (such as succeeding in school and helping others),
- less likely to get into trouble (such as hitting someone or threatening to physically harm someone), and

- more likely to bounce back from difficulty (such as a serious illness or the death of a loved one).

I was impressed with these three outcomes. These are things I wanted for my children. I've been parenting with the Developmental Assets framework ever since.

Using the Developmental Assets Framework to Parent Your Child Well

The first time you examine the Developmental Assets framework, think of the list of items as essential nutrients for healthy development. While your child may not experience every asset all the time, you want to provide a consistent balance of as many different nutrients as possible. When you are intentional about giving a young person these experiences, you are *asset building*.

As you read through the list, the first thing you'll see is that there are 40 Developmental Assets. Don't panic! Forty may seem like a lot, but those 40 assets actually overlap each other in everyday life.

Remember that while you may be trying to build one specific asset, you're often building other assets at the same time. For example, when you read aloud a picture book to your preschooler before bed, you're building asset 25: early literacy, as well as asset 2: positive family communication, and asset 20: time at home. One effort from you can have multiple positive results for your preschooler.

Because the assets can seem like a "to-do" list with 40 items, I found it less daunting to start by reflecting on how the eight broad categories relate to parenting:
- Support
- Empowerment

- Boundaries and expectations
- Constructive use of time
- Commitment to learning
- Positive values
- Social competencies
- Positive identity

The first four categories (support, empowerment, boundaries and expectations, and constructive use of time) are external assets. These assets are built through families, preschools, friends, neighborhoods, congregations, and community organizations. In many ways, they're the easiest assets to build because they're about forming relationships and exposing preschoolers to high-quality programs and activities.

The last four categories (commitment to learning, positive values, social competencies, and positive identity) are internal assets—the commitments, passions, and values we want to instill in our children. We can do this through modeling and teaching, and we can also give preschoolers a lot of opportunities to develop their character.

When I first tried asset building, I started with the category of support. I began being more intentional about how I supported my preschool-age children. I quickly became aware that my two children wanted different types of support from me. My son liked having me nearby—but not too close. If I tried to hold his hand when we went to the zoo, he resisted (and sometimes very loudly). Once I began letting him explore on his own (while keeping a close eye on him nearby), he was much more content. I was surprised when he eventually started running back to me, grabbing my hand, and showing me the meerkats and the ring-tailed lemurs.

My daughter was the opposite. As a preschooler she spent a lot of time in my lap or standing next to me and holding my hand (or clutching it when she was afraid). In talking with other parents, I've learned that they, too, have noticed differences in their preschool-age children. Sometimes it was the boy who was cuddly and the girl who wanted more distance. Other times, it was something else, such as the preschooler who felt supported only when he was allowed to carry a dead battery everywhere he went! Basic temperament can vary widely even among children raised by the same parents. You may not understand all of your child's behaviors or developmental needs, but focusing on the eight asset categories can help you tune in to what matters to your preschooler.

Over time, I learned more about the Developmental Assets framework and the common sense wisdom it offered. I started simply by hanging a photocopy of the list on my refrigerator, and the Developmental Assets approach gradually became second nature to me. I began building each one intentionally with my children. Now every time I parent, I focus on building assets.

What This Book Offers

Parenting Preschoolers with a Purpose is a practical, easy-to-use guide for building assets while parenting your preschooler. This book offers a variety of ways to ground yourself when your head begins to spin and you fear that you're not giving your child what she needs to grow up well.

If you are interested in learning more about Developmental Assets and exploring each of the eight categories, Part 1 of this book delves more deeply into asset-building parenting. Who are the other people who can best support—and become advocates for—your child? How do you teach your child values when he puts up resistance? Which activities are best for your child? Here's where you'll find the answers to these questions—and more.

Part 2 focuses on taking care of yourself as a parent. Because you're more effective as a parent when you team up with other caring adults, this book includes helpful ideas on how to create a web of support for yourself as well as your child. Part 2 explores an alphabetical list of issues such as boredom, guilt, job demands, stress, and taking breaks from parenting so that you can feel good about yourself as an individual and as a parent. When you begin to build assets intentionally with your child and team up with other caring adults in your child's life, you'll make a big impact in the long run—even if your everyday efforts initially seem small or insignificant.

How do you get a picky eater to eat a more varied, healthy diet? How do you calm down an intense preschooler who is always energetic and crashing into everything? What if your 3-year-old stops napping? What if your 5-year-old still sucks his thumb? If you're simply looking for helpful ideas or quick tips for troubleshooting the daily experience of parenting a preschooler, turn to the third section of the book. Organized alphabetically, Part 3 offers concrete asset-building ideas for 40 common situations.

Throughout this book, the words *parent* and *parents* refer to the adult or a group of adults who are doing the primary job of raising a child. Many children do not live with two biological parents, or even one. Rather than repeatedly listing all the possible ways you can parent (biological parent, single parent, stepparent, guardian, adoptive parent, foster parent, grandparents raising grand-children, working parent, stay-at-home parent, etc.), the terms *parent* and *parents* are intended to include all types of family structures. If you're caring for and raising a child, you *are* a parent, and this book is for you.

A Step in the Right Direction

If you're struggling with how to parent a preschooler and finding that it isn't always easy, rest assured that you're probably doing a lot of things right. The trick is figuring out how to maneuver through the bumps, battles, and baffling maze of parenting a preschooler so that both you and your child can learn and grow together.

Look no further. *Parenting Preschoolers with a Purpose* will help you survive these fun but frustrating years. All you have to do is take one step, one small step at a time. Choose one simple thing you can do. Maybe you'll model peaceful conflict resolution when you disagree with a neighbor. Or maybe you'll start taking a class with your preschooler. Or maybe you'll dust off that instrument you used to play and perform for your child while she dances.

Any small step makes a difference, and every step mat-ters. Parenting is a journey with many unexpected twists and turns, and although some of the twists will aggravate you, others will make you laugh. Try to have fun and enjoy the journey while you keep learning asset-building ways to care for your child and yourself. As you become intentional about using the Developmental Assets frame-work, you'll find that, before long, you really are parent-ing with a purpose.

PART 1

*Becoming an
Asset-Building Parent*

Parenting with the Asset Framework

It's easy to get swept up in the problem of the day. Oh, my! My son refuses to eat any vegetables. Oh, no! My daughter keeps waking up at night and wanting to sleep with me. Oh, dear! My preschooler is bouncing off the walls!

SPOTLIGHT ON ASSETS

The 40 Developmental Assets

At first it may seem overwhelming to focus on all 40 Developmental Assets to parent your preschooler well. The complete list appears on pages 7–11, but you may find it less intimidating to focus on the eight categories of assets:

1. Support
2. Empowerment
3. Boundaries and expectations
4. Constructive use of time
5. Commitment to learning
6. Positive values
7. Social competencies
8. Positive identity

This first section of the book will highlight each category and give you concrete suggestions for incorporating asset building into your parenting. As you become more familiar with asset building over time, you can begin to delve into each of the 40 assets.

Child-development experts contend that the acting-out behavior of preschoolers is normal. "You will feel less hopeless and less angry if you can keep in mind that behaving in an out-of-bounds manner is not only an almost inevitable but probably a quite necessary part of [preschool] development," suggest researchers from the Gesell Institute of Human Development. They say the most difficult times during the preschool years tend to happen when a child is 3½, 4½, and 5½.

The truth is, you will encounter problems in parenting your child, and you will continue to stumble into new difficulties as your child grows up. If you continue to keep your focus only on the problems that come along, you'll become a reactive parent instead of a purposeful parent.

All parents want their children to grow up well and to succeed. To guide your child along this positive path requires having a practical parenting framework that helps you to be intentional—a road map that helps you clarify what you need to do to raise healthy, caring children.

Search Institute's Developmental Assets framework can offer this perspective. Research on more than two million young people across North America makes it clear that children and teenagers with more Developmental Assets are:

- More likely to act in ways we value (such as exhibiting leadership and maintaining good health habits);
- Less likely to get into trouble (such as hurting someone or becoming depressed); and
- More likely to bounce back when life gets hard and bad things happen.

David builds assets. He says he now reads a picture book to his son each night before going to bed, and he feels closer to his son because they have this time together. Gina builds assets by taking an anger-management class. She used to yell and hit her child, but she doesn't anymore. Hector builds assets by coaching a preschool soccer team in his community, and his 4-year-old daughter thinks he's the best soccer coach ever. Deshona builds assets by playing games with her son every day.

What about you?

Some of the examples listed above probably seem like common sense, but the Developmental Assets framework gives you a proven, practical approach to parenting preschoolers. Not only will it help your child succeed, but it also will make your job as a parent easier. Instead of always dealing with problems, you'll be creating a positive home atmosphere where both you and your preschooler will thrive.

Asset-Building Parenting Ideas

Whenever you try something new, start with something easy. Become an asset-building parent with these ideas:

1. Learn more about the Developmental Assets framework. Download a copy of the Developmental Assets for Early Childhood by visiting www.search-institute.org/assets/assetlists.html. Post a copy in your home. Carry another copy with you and periodically read it when you're stuck waiting in line at a store.

2. Scan the list of 40 Developmental Assets and focus on one asset that you can begin building in your child. For example, you might choose asset 23: home-program connection, and become more intentional about connecting with adults at your child's preschool and extracurricular activities.

3. Periodically consult the list of 40 Developmental Assets and choose a new asset (from another category) to use in your parenting. For example, if you chose asset 23: home-program connection, from the commitment-to-learning category as your first asset, choose an asset from another category, such as asset 4: caring neighbors, from the support category. Over time, be intentional about building an asset from each of the eight categories.

4. Connect with other parents about what works. Compare parenting ideas and strategies. Tell them about Developmental Assets and how the framework is helping you as a parent.

5. Find another asset-building resource that helps you become a more intentional, asset-building parent. See the resource list on page 205 for ideas.

External Assets

SUPPORT

1. **Family support**—Parent(s) and/or primary caregiver(s) provide the child with high levels of consistent and predictable love, physical care, and positive attention in ways that are responsive to the child's individuality.
2. **Positive family communication**—Parent(s) and/or primary caregiver(s) express themselves positively and respectfully, engaging young children in conversations that invite their input.
3. **Other adult relationships**—With the family's support, the child experiences consistent, caring relationships with adults outside the family.
4. **Caring neighbors**—The child's network of relationships includes neighbors who provide emotional support and a sense of belonging.
5. **Caring climate in child-care and educational settings**—Caregivers and teachers create environments that are nurturing, accepting, encouraging, and secure.
6. **Parent involvement in child care and education**—Parent(s), caregivers, and teachers together create a consistent and supportive approach to fostering the child's successful growth.

EMPOWERMENT

7. **Community cherishes and values young children**—Children are welcomed and included throughout community life.
8. **Children seen as resources**—The community demonstrates that children are valuable resources by investing in a child-rearing system of family support and high-quality activities and resources to meet children's physical, social, and emotional needs.

9. **Service to others**—The child has opportunities to perform simple but meaningful and caring actions for others.
10. **Safety**—Parent(s), caregivers, teachers, neighbors, and the community take action to ensure children's health and safety.

BOUNDARIES AND EXPECTATIONS

11. **Family boundaries**—The family provides consistent supervision for the child and maintains reasonable guidelines for behavior that the child can understand and achieve.
12. **Boundaries in child-care and educational settings**—Caregivers and educators use positive approaches to discipline and natural consequences to encourage self-regulation and acceptable behaviors.
13. **Neighborhood boundaries**—Neighbors encourage the child in positive, acceptable behavior, as well as intervene in negative behavior, in a supportive, nonthreatening way.
14. **Adult role models**—Parent(s), caregivers, and other adults model self-control, social skills, engagement in learning, and healthy lifestyles.
15. **Positive peer relationships**—Parent(s) and caregivers seek to provide opportunities for the child to interact positively with other children.
16. **Positive expectations**—Parent(s), caregivers, and teachers encourage and support the child in behaving appropriately, undertaking challenging tasks, and performing activities to the best of her or his abilities.

CONSTRUCTIVE USE OF TIME

17. **Play and creative activities**—The child has daily opportunities to play in ways that allow self-expression, physical activity, and interaction with others.

18. **Out-of-home and community programs**—The child experiences well-designed programs led by competent, caring adults in well-maintained settings.
19. **Religious community**—The child participates in age-appropriate religious activities and caring relationships that nurture her or his spiritual development.
20. **Time at home**—The child spends most of her or his time at home participating in family activities and playing constructively, with parent(s) guiding TV and electronic game use.

Internal Assets

COMMITMENT TO LEARNING

21. **Motivation to mastery**—The child responds to new experiences with curiosity and energy, resulting in the pleasure of mastering new learning and skills.
22. **Engagement in learning experiences**—The child fully participates in a variety of activities that offer opportunities for learning.
23. **Home-program connection**—The child experiences security, consistency, and connections between home and out-of-home care programs and learning activities.
24. **Bonding to programs**—The child forms meaningful connections with out-of-home care and educational programs.
25. **Early literacy**—The child enjoys a variety of pre-reading activities, including adults reading to her or him daily, looking at and handling books, playing with a variety of media, and showing interest in pictures, letters, and numbers.

POSITIVE VALUES

26. **Caring**—The child begins to show empathy, understanding, and awareness of others' feelings.
27. **Equality and social justice**—The child begins to show concern for people who are excluded from play and other activities or not treated fairly because they are different.
28. **Integrity**—The child begins to express her or his views appropriately and to stand up for a growing sense of what is fair and right.
29. **Honesty**—The child begins to understand the difference between truth and lies, and is truthful to the extent of her or his understanding.
30. **Responsibility**—The child begins to follow through on simple tasks to take care of her- or himself and to help others.
31. **Self-regulation**—The child increasingly can identify, regulate, and control her or his behaviors in healthy ways, using adult support constructively in particularly stressful situations.

SOCIAL COMPETENCIES

32. **Planning and decision making**—The child begins to plan for the immediate future, choosing from among several options and trying to solve problems.
33. **Interpersonal skills**—The child cooperates, shares, plays harmoniously, and comforts others in distress.
34. **Cultural awareness and sensitivity**—The child begins to learn about her or his own cultural identity and to show acceptance of people who are racially, physically, culturally, or ethnically different from her or him.

35. **Resistance skills**—The child begins to sense danger accurately, to seek help from trusted adults, and to resist pressure from peers to participate in unacceptable or risky behavior.

36. **Peaceful conflict resolution**—The child begins to compromise and resolve conflicts without using physical aggression or hurtful language.

POSITIVE IDENTITY

37. **Personal power**—The child can make choices that give a sense of having some influence over things that happen in her or his life.

38. **Self-esteem**—The child likes her- or himself and has a growing sense of being valued by others.

39. **Sense of purpose**—The child anticipates new opportunities, experiences, and milestones in growing up.

40. **Positive view of personal future**—The child finds the world interesting and enjoyable, and feels that he or she has a positive place in it.

Support

One key aspect of asset building centers around support. Preschoolers thrive when they feel supported, and they're more likely to continue making other important firsts (such as sleeping overnight at Grandma's, going to a friend's to play, and taking a school bus to kindergarten) when they feel the adults around them care about them and are cheering them on.

> **SPOTLIGHT ON ASSETS**
>
> *The Support Assets: Assets 1–6*
>
> Children grow up well when they feel supported and cared for by their parents and other people around them. Search Institute has identified six support assets that make a difference in the lives of preschoolers.
>
> 1. Family support
> 2. Positive family communication
> 3. Other adult relationships
> 4. Caring neighbors
> 5. Caring climate in child-care and educational settings
> 6. Parent involvement in child care and education

As an asset-building parent, you want to create a network of support for yourself and your child. Some of those supports will be the same, but others will be different. Be intentional about creating these networks so that you know who you can go to and who will be an advocate for your child.

In Santa Clara County, California, more than 200 parents are involved in small asset-building groups where they get to know each other and learn to parent using the Developmental Assets framework. These parents have become advocates for their children and for each other.

Although it takes a while to create a network of support, the first step is to find one person who cares about parenting like you. Once you have a supportive partner, parenting becomes much easier because you know someone believes in you and what you're doing.

Asset-Building Parenting Ideas
Support is always around us. The problem is that we often don't know it. Try these asset-building ideas to connect with your child and build your family's network of support:

1. Introduce yourself to other parents of preschoolers. Get to know their names and which children they're connected to.

2. Be creative in developing a network of support. Some parents connect through e-mail since family schedules make it difficult to get together on a regular basis.

3. Examine all your relationships to create a network of support. Are there people in your extended family who are supportive? Friends? Neighbors? People who attend your congregation? Coworkers? Caregivers? Teachers? Other parents? One single parent discovered an elderly man at her congregation who took a liking to her son. He became a significant support to both of them.

4. If you travel for work or have joint custody of your children, create a short letter for your child to open each day you're apart. One parent always drew a silly picture. Another occasionally included a phone card and a joke.

5. Whenever you're dropping off or picking up your child for child care or another program, greet and talk with other parents who are coming at the same time.

BONUS IDEA

Get-Together Meals

Have three to four families with preschoolers get together to eat so you can get to know each other better. To keep the kids stimulated, have one or two adults play with the children in a separate area while the rest of the adults talk. After 15 minutes, have another adult or two relieve the first set of adults. Continue in 15-minute cycles until the end of your time together. That way you'll get more adult conversation, the kids will get plenty of attention, and the adults will also get to know each other's kids.

Empowerment

When children are cherished and valued, they're more likely to develop into healthy individuals. Empowering preschoolers can be as simple as giving them small tasks that they can succeed at, and it can be as complex as a group of parents starting an asset-based community initiative that values children and families.

To empower your child, regularly give your child opportunities to help and do her best. At mealtimes, preschoolers can tear up lettuce for salads, fold napkins and set them next to each place, and carry their used plate to the kitchen afterward. If you have a pet, your child can help feed the pet or go on walks with your dog (with adult supervision).

SPOTLIGHT ON ASSETS

The Empowerment Assets: Assets 7–10

Children who feel valued and valuable are empowered to help others and to develop in ways that help them become well-rounded, healthy individuals. Search Institute has named four empowerment assets that help young children grow up well:

   7. Community cherishes and values young children
   8. Children seen as resources
   9. Service to others
   10. Safety

Playtimes also empower preschoolers when they have toys and materials that stimulate their thinking and encourage them to learn new skills without becoming overly frustrated or bored. Some parents rotate toys so that old toys are put away and then pulled out months later. Other parents create toy exchanges with other families so that they don't have to buy as many toys and children get the chance to try something new.

Asset-Building Parenting Ideas

Empowering your child helps him to feel cherished and valued. Try these asset-building ideas to empower yourself and your child:

1. Preschoolers love simple puzzles, so create a puzzle out of a helpful chore. Purchase an inexpensive paper table cloth and outline a place setting (plate, cup, spoon, knife, fork, and napkin) at each person's spot. Then have your preschooler put the puzzle together by setting the table.

2. Empower your child to help you at the grocery store by creating five index cards (each one with a clipped magazine photo of foods you regularly buy from different grocery sections). Give your child the cards to find the items at the store as you shop together. For example, you might have cards that show: a milk carton, bananas, a box of cereal, chicken, and ice cream. As a reward for finding the five items, some parents let their child choose one treat to buy.

3. Create a pictorial phone book for your preschooler. On each page, put a person's photo and the phone number in large, easy-to-read numbers. Include grandparents, favorite family members, and friends. Sit with your child and watch her or him dial the numbers when calling. Coach your child in how to greet someone, tell who's calling, and how to end a phone call.

BONUS IDEA

Hopping for a Good Cause

Children between the ages of 2 and 6 can participate in the Muscular Dystrophy Association's (MDA) annual Hop-a-Thon®. Children and their parents collect pledges, and children not only hop for a good cause but also learn more about disabilities. Children are empowered to make a difference by doing something they're good at: hopping. Check out www.mdausa.org in the United States or www.muscle.ca in Canada for more information.

---

4. When your child has a date to play at a friend's home, explain that your child needs to follow the safety rules of that family. If your child returns home confused about why you let her play outside and the other family doesn't, explain why you have your safety rule while another family may not have the same rule. For example, your child's friend may live on a busier street than you do—or the friend may have recently run into the street. Then point out that everyone can still get along even if they have different opinions and rules.

5. Develop a weekly job chart for your child. List simple tasks, such as putting dirty clothes into a hamper or down a clothes chute; putting away clean spoons, forks, and knives from the dishwasher; dusting the television; and picking up toys off the floor. Have your child place a star (or sticker) next to each task completed for that day. At the end of the week, give money (such as a penny or a nickel) for each star.

Boundaries & Expectations

Preschoolers do not develop well if they are only supported and empowered. They also need clear boundaries set for them that are consistently reinforced. This involves teaching children what's out of bounds (responding to conflicts with hitting and swearing is not acceptable) and what's in bounds (helping others and working hard in preschool). We also expect a lot from our kids, knowing that high expectations help them grow.

As parents, we set boundaries and hold high expectations at home. We also need, however, to connect with other places in our children's lives (such as neighbors,

---

SPOTLIGHT ON ASSETS

The Boundaries-and-Expectations Assets: Assets 11–16

Giving children clear, appropriate guidelines and expectations helps them know what to expect and how to act. These six boundaries-and-expectations assets help young children develop into well-rounded individuals:

11. Family boundaries
12. Boundaries in child-care and educational settings
13. Neighborhood boundaries
14. Adult role models
15. Positive peer relationships
16. Positive expectations

---

child-care centers, preschools, and faith communities) so that they also set boundaries consistent with the boundaries parents set at home.

When children know what to expect, they're more likely to know how to behave. Being clear about behaviors and what we want for our children goes a long way toward helping them make positive choices to grow up well.

Asset-Building Parenting Ideas

Setting clear boundaries and expectations is only one aspect of building the six assets in this area. Children also need positive role models and strong friendships. Try these asset-building ideas:

1. Create a friendship bulletin board or poster for your child. Include a photo of each of your child's friends along with the name written under each photo. Make the friendship board intergenerational. Include grandpas, grandmas, aunts, uncles, and favorite neighbors in addition to peers. Hang the friendship poster in your child's room.

2. To motivate preschoolers to pick up after a playdate, create a thank-you jar of candy, stickers, super balls, and other small (inexpensive) toys. Fifteen minutes before a friend is to be picked up, have the children clean up the room and choose a thank-you surprise from the jar after they finish.

3. If you have joint custody of your child with another parent and your child has to master different daily routines, create a picture card reminder so that he knows what to expect at each home. For example, if your child attends a child care or preschool four days a week, and you split the pick-up days with the other parent, create

Give Preschoolers Consistent Messages

One of the difficulties about parenting is that children receive different sets of rules depending on where they are. (And as a parent, it's also tempting to create longer lists of rules as your child discovers new areas of trouble.) Ask for the lists of rules from the adults at the places where you child spends time, such as a child-care center, preschool, congregation education program, or community program. Have the same rules at home. For programs that don't have rules, advocate that they adopt a list consistent with other programs. Child-care centers, Montessori schools, and preschools often have short, easy-to-follow lists of rules that address a wide range of behavior.

a laminated index card with your photo and another card with the other parent's photo. Give the laminated index card with your picture to your child on the days you pick him up. Send the other card with your child on the other days. If your child is confused about who's coming to get him, all he has to do is peek at the card.

4. Meet with other neighbors in your neighborhood and set neighborhood boundaries for children. For example, some neighborhoods allow children to play in certain areas, such as in the apartments of specific families or in the front yards of specified neighbors. In other neighborhoods, residents agree to intervene when children misbehave and show them better ways to act.

5. Create a game out of a nonnegotiable boundary to help enforce it. For example, most preschoolers resist taking prescribed medicine. (Many can taste the medicine despite the added flavor.) Since sick preschoolers need to take their medicine, make a game to enforce this boundary. Let your child choose a favorite beverage, such as orange or grape juice (the stronger the taste, the better). Pour one small glass for your child and two for yourself. Have your child race you in taking the medicine before gulping down the juice while you drink the two cups. (Make sure your child wins.)

Constructive Use of Time

How children spend their time greatly contributes to—
or hinders—their development. Most parents control how
preschoolers spend their time, and it's essential to make
wise choices so that children grow up well. Children need
developmentally appropriate, enticing programs run by
principled, caring adults. These can be drama activities,
sports teams, clubs, religious groups, music lessons, and
stimulating time spent at home.

SPOTLIGHT ON ASSETS

The Constructive-Use-of-Time Assets:
Assets 17–20

What children do with their time makes a difference.
Search Institute researchers have discovered that a
number of activities help young people develop into
successful, healthy adults. The four constructive-use-
of-time assets include:

17. Play and creative activities
18. Out-of-home and community programs
19. Religious community
20. Time at home

What's lacking for many kids, however, is having
proper supervision and meaningful, stimulating activities.
Although preschoolers are more independent than infants
and toddlers, they still need consistent adult supervision
to ensure their safety.

As parents, we play an important role in helping our children discover enriching activities that tap their interests, stimulate their growth, and nurture their spirit. We also help them make choices so that they don't become consumed and overcommitted. When preschoolers spend their time well, they're much more likely to grow up well and succeed.

Asset-Building Parenting Ideas

The way preschoolers spend all of their time—whether at home or in different settings—matters. Give preschoolers stimulating, worthwhile activities that help them grow. Try these ideas to build the constructive-use-of-time assets in your child:

1. Create a collection of PVC piping and joints (available at any building-supply store) and help your child create a fort, playhouse, cave, or tent by draping blankets over the frames you construct. This helps to stimulate your child's imagination and gives her another interesting place to play.

2. If you live in a snowy climate, make snow faces with your preschooler on the side of the house, garage, or tree. Mound up small snowballs to make two eyes and a nose and stick the snow onto your house. (Tell your preschooler to think of the house as the head.) Then create a mouth with a longer strip of snow. Older preschoolers will enjoy making hair and other body parts.

3. If your family attends worship services at a congregation, create an activity bag for your child to use only during worship. Include paper, washable markers, a coloring book, and a picture book (or two). Ask your child to do these activities quietly when he seems restless. At home, encourage your child to play worship. If you're Buddhist, your child might create an offertory box near the door for donations. If you're Jewish, have your child create a *tzedakah* box to drop coins in. If you're Christian, give your child envelopes to use as offering envelopes and a large plastic plate or bucket to use as an offering plate. Have your child use stuffed animals to act the roles of various religious leaders who participate in worship.

BONUS IDEA

Create a Neighborhood Art Gallery

Invite children from your neighborhood to create art for a neighborhood art gallery. Display the gallery outside in the summer or in someone's garage or home on an uncooperative weather day. Invite neighbors for the viewing (and have snacks and drinks available). Don't be surprised if some neighbors want to buy some artwork.

---

4. Let your preschooler become a Picasso. Take a paper plate. Squeeze small paint blobs (one circle for each color) around the perimeter of the plate. Let your child mix her own paint colors in the middle like artists do. You may need to create replacement plates since most preschoolers will mix all the colors the first time. With other plates, guide your child's mixing by asking: What happens if you mix only blue and yellow?

5. Take your Mr. and Mrs. Potato Head® set with you to the beach (or out in the snow). Instead of using the potato as the head, use a mound of sand (or snow). Preschoolers will become quite innovative with the faces they create.

Commitment to Learning

Infants and toddlers are naturally curious, and keeping this curiosity alive is a critical task of parents. "As [children] progress to and through the primary grades, a great many lose their natural curiosity and enthusiasm for learning," concluded the Carnegie Task Force on Learning in the Primary Grades.

Preschoolers whose parents are involved in their education, whose parents are enthusiastic about learning in general, and whose parents create a home environment that encourages learning earn higher grades than children whose parents don't make these choices. This level of active commitment to learning is just as important (or more so) as children become more independent and make more of their own choices about education and learning. Cultivating these commitment-to-learning assets is critical for your child's success in learning and in life.

SPOTLIGHT ON ASSETS

The Commitment-to-Learning Assets:
Assets 21–25

Five Developmental Assets make up the category of commitment to learning. These assets are:

    21. Motivation to mastery
    22. Engagement in learning experiences
    23. Home-program connection
    24. Bonding to programs
    25. Early literacy

Asset-Building Parenting Ideas

Keep your child's curiosity alive and growing. Try these asset-building ideas to instill a commitment to learning in your child:

1. To help preschoolers learn their numbers, occasionally let them dial a phone number for you under your close supervision. Preschoolers feel proud when they find the matching digits and dial the correct number.

2. If your child attends a preschool or child-care center, volunteer as a "Reading Dad" or a "Reading Mom" once a month (or a few times a year). Schedule a time with teachers or caregivers to come in and read aloud picture books to the children.

BONUS IDEA

Your Star Reader

Every time you read aloud a book to your child and your child pays full attention, draw a star on a piece of paper and write the name of the book on the star. Hang the star on your child's bedroom door or wall. When there are 25 stars, take your child to the used bookstore to choose one picture book to buy.

---

3. To teach basic math skills, such as recognizing similarities between items and placing them into sets, give your preschooler a bag of mixed dried beans. (Make sure you don't have any younger children around who might try to put the beans into their mouths.) Place an empty egg carton in front of your child and ask her or him to sort the beans. If your child is excited about numbers, write the numbers 1 to 12 on the bottom of an empty egg carton (with one number—in order—in each spot). Give your child M&M's® or jelly beans. Ask your child to place the same amount of candy in each spot to match the number.

4. To help your child feel more attached to her preschool or child-care center, display class pictures in your home. If center T-shirts are for sale, buy one for your child to wear. Use whatever items the center offers (from mugs to bags) to show your support and enthusiasm.

5. Have your child choose a number between 1 and 10 to be the number of the day. Then incorporate that number into the activities and routines of your day. For example, if your child chooses the number six, have your child wear six ponytails in her hair. Have snacks cut into six pieces (such as apples). Let your child choose six toys to take into the bathtub. Kiss your child six times before bed.

Positive Values

Building character involves teaching children important internal compasses that guide them in making choices. Search Institute identified six positive values based on various research studies: caring, equality and social justice, integrity, honesty, responsibility, and self-regulation. The first two assets relate to the prosocial values of caring for others and for the world. The other four values address the area of personal character. These four values provide a foundation that allows preschoolers to make wise, compassionate decisions.

SPOTLIGHT ON ASSETS

The Positive-Values Assets: Assets 26–31

Search Institute has identified these positive values as Developmental Assets:
- 26. Caring
- 27. Equality and social justice
- 28. Integrity
- 29. Honesty
- 30. Responsibility
- 31. Self-regulation

Teaching children positive values takes a long time. While you model these values, it's also important to teach them to your children. As they grow older, it's also helpful to explain why these values are important: "Honest people are people you can trust." "People who value equality make the world a better place." "When you take responsibility, people can depend on you."

The categories of positive values and boundaries and expectations go hand in hand. When you intervene and tell a preschooler not to hit, not only are you giving a clear boundary, but you're also teaching children to care for others and to take responsibility for their actions.

Asset-Building Parenting Ideas

Instilling positive values in your child requires intentional parenting. Besides teaching your child values, also jump on teachable moments to emphasize why positive values are important. Try these asset-building ideas:

1. Even though it's much easier and more efficient for you alone to bake cookies for someone who's in the hospital, make cookies together with your preschooler. Ask your preschooler to draw a picture on a card. Then deliver the cookies and card to the hospital together.

2. With your preschooler, volunteer at a soup kitchen or homeless shelter so your child can see people who don't have as much as your family has. It's helpful to choose projects that actually put you face-to-face with the recipient; volunteer service that keeps the recipient hidden can be too abstract for young children. For example, a preschooler may grasp the concept of dishing up food at a shelter better than donating canned goods to a food bank.

3. Whenever your child wants to help another child (such as console a crying child), encourage your child to act on that impulse. This teaches children how to act on positive values that they have strong feelings about.

4. When your child is honest (especially when it's hard for him to tell the truth but he does so anyway), praise your child. Catch him acting in positive ways and tell him how proud you are.

5. Create an in-box for each family member by writing the name of each family member on a separate box. Have a pick-up time each evening when family members line up the boxes in the middle of the room and sort items strewn around the room. Place each item into the appropriate owner's box. (Preschoolers enjoy doing this, especially when they're not the only ones who leave out items.) When everything is picked up, ask family members to take their own boxes to their rooms and put away their items.

Social Competencies

Social competencies are the skills preschoolers need when they encounter problems and other life situations. These specific skills help them deal with the choices, challenges, and opportunities they face in building and maintaining relationships with others.

Social competencies give children tools to live out their values, beliefs, and priorities. Although preschoolers are young and have not fully developed these concepts, they learn about these things through their parents and other adults around them. Social competencies are also vital to forming the kinds of positive, supportive relationships they need.

For parents, then, teaching these essential skills over and over as children grow is vital, knowing that our chil-

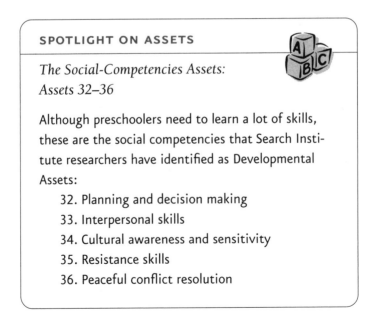

SPOTLIGHT ON ASSETS

The Social-Competencies Assets:
Assets 32–36

Although preschoolers need to learn a lot of skills, these are the social competencies that Search Institute researchers have identified as Developmental Assets:

32. Planning and decision making
33. Interpersonal skills
34. Cultural awareness and sensitivity
35. Resistance skills
36. Peaceful conflict resolution

dren continue expanding—and relying on—their network of friendships as they grow older. Specific competencies, such as planning and decision making and peaceful conflict resolution, develop over the course of many years, even decades.

Asset-Building Parenting Ideas

To teach your preschooler social competencies, try these asset-building ideas:

1. Once a month, have your child choose a book about another country. Serve a meal from that country. Learn a few words (such as hello, good-bye, and thank you) spoken in the country's major language. If possible, play a game or learn a song from that country. This shows preschoolers about the value of different cultures through first-hand exposure.

2. To teach healthy eating habits while giving preschoolers the power to choose their food, create a chart that includes your child's favorite fruits and vegetables. If you want your child to eat five servings a day while having only one unhealthy snack (which you might want to call a fun food), say that he can have the fun food once the five fruits and vegetables are eaten that day. Let your child choose which fruit or vegetable to eat and mark it off on the chart. Make sure you're stocked up with these foods and eat them along with your child to model what you teach.

3. Create family activities on major holidays that give your preschooler the opportunity to interact with extended family members and guests. For example, cut out construction-paper turkey feathers and have your pre-

A Jar of Great Choices

Sometimes preschoolers get bored. When they do, it's helpful to have several activity options they can choose from (which helps them learn about making decisions). With your preschooler, talk about all the favorite activities he enjoys. For example, your child may say painting, going to the library, visiting the neighbor's dog, or popping popcorn. Feel free to suggest ideas, but let your child decide which ideas go into the jar. Write each activity on a separate piece of paper. Fold each paper and place it in a jar. The next time your child is looking for something interesting to do, pull out the jar and let him make a choice to conquer boredom.

schooler ask each guest to write one thing she is thankful for on Thanksgiving. Display the feathers next to a construction-paper turkey on the wall.

4. You want your child to resist danger—but not resist every transition he needs to make throughout the day. Since preschoolers have a hard time changing from one activity to another, give him a five-minute warning. Some parents use an egg timer (which gives about a three-minute warning) as a visual reminder in addition to their spoken word.

5. When your child gets into a conflict with another child, have the children stop and do three things:

1) name their feeling (for example: mad), 2) say why they have that feeling (for example: she stole my toy), and 3) say and do one thing to calm down (for example: walk away and find a book to look at). Each time your child gets into a conflict, repeat those three steps. After a while, your child will automatically start to do these three steps without your reminder.

Positive Identity

Many parents think of nurturing their child's self-esteem as the way to build a positive identity, yet it involves much more than that. Helping preschoolers figure out who they are, what they can do, and who they want to become is a critical task that requires helping them gain a sense of personal power, a sense of purpose, and a positive view of the future, in addition to a high self-esteem. Although children won't fully figure out these aspects of themselves until they are much older, you can lay the foundation for them on which to build their sense of self.

SPOTLIGHT ON ASSETS

The Positive-Identity Assets:
Assets 37–40

A strong personal identity is more than positive self-esteem. Search Institute researchers have identified four Developmental Assets in the area of positive identity. They include:

37. Personal power
38. Self-esteem
39. Sense of purpose
40. Positive view of personal future

Your child will change dramatically between the ages of 3 and 5, and a lot of that change is due to your child's sense of identity. During the preschool years, children become aware that they are separate individuals, and they begin to realize that you have feelings just like they do.

In fact, it's quite touching when your preschooler comes up to you for the first time and consoles you when you're upset. By fostering positive identity with your child, you open the door for these wonderful personality traits to take shape.

Asset-Building Parenting Ideas

Nurturing a strong identity in your child is much more than paying attention to her and praising the positive things she does. Try these ideas to build a strong identity in your preschooler:

1. If your child misses you while he goes to child care, attends an activity, or is with a baby-sitter, give your child a photograph of yourself. Tell him to look at the photo whenever he misses you. (Some parents fill their child's pocket full of blown kisses and tell their child to take out a kiss whenever the child feels lonely.) Helping your child with loneliness while you're away helps to build your child's self-identity.

2. When your child celebrates her birthday, extend the celebration to the entire birth week. Take your child out one-on-one to her favorite restaurant (or out for ice cream). At mealtimes, talk about your child's birth story or adoption arrival story. Tell what you like best about your child.

3. Keep a notebook for each of your children. Whenever your child says (or does) something funny or profound, write it down. Every so often, take out the notebook and read aloud stories about your child. Your child will love hearing these stories, and the notebook will become a treasured keepsake when he is older. You can similarly record these memories on a calendar, which makes it even easier to jot down daily thoughts as they come to you.

4. Young preschoolers like to put on their own shoes, but they often place them on the wrong feet. Draw a picture of an animal (such as a cat or dog) on the bottoms of the shoes, with the head and front feet drawn on the sole of the left shoe and the rest of the body and back feet drawn on the sole of the right shoe. Have your child put the picture together (which places the shoes in the correct position) before putting on her or his shoes.

BONUS IDEA

The Power of Your Child's Name

Plant a garden with your child that reveals your child's first name as the plants grow. Outline your child's name in the dirt (at the proper depth according to the seed package) and plant seeds, such as radishes or beans. As the plants appear, so does your child's name. You can also do this with a pumpkin. When the pumpkin is small, lightly carve your child's name on the pumpkin with a knife. As the pumpkin grows, so does your child's name.

---

5. A key aspect of building a child's identity is having your child master skills. Children between the ages of 3 and 5 practice a lot of skills and gradually master them. For example, children can typically roll a ball between the ages of 2 and 4, hop on one foot by age 3, kick a stationary ball at age 3, throw a ball underarm between the ages of 3 and 4, skip by age 4, catch a ball by trapping it along the chest at age 4, throw a ball overarm between the ages of 4 and 5, catch a ball with hands at age 5, and kick a rolling ball at age 5 or 6. Whenever your child masters a new skill (even if it's somewhat rudimentary), notice it and say how proud you are of your child. Delight in the new skills your child is learning.

PART 2

~

*Taking Care
of Yourself*

Adult Relationships

When you become a parent, you may see rapid changes in the relationships you have with other adults. Yes, some relationships remain, but typically many parents see their adult social networks shift.

During your child's infancy, you probably saw some of your relationships drift away. As a parent, you were busy and could no longer spend as much time with certain people. If some of your friends were single or married without children, they may have turned their energy toward adults who were more like them: adults without children.

Of the adults who remained in your life, most likely you noticed other changes. Your relationship with your parents and extended family began to shift because of the addition of your child. If you were married or in a committed relationship, that relationship also began to change. Researcher John Gottman contends there are three major marital stress points: when the first child is three months old, after the birth of a second child, and when the first child becomes a teenager. Making these observations in the October 1997 issue of *The Atlantic*, Gottman contends that 70 percent of couples could be helped so that they have more meaningful marriages and family lives.

What does that research finding have to do with parenting preschoolers? A lot. You may be in the middle of the second or third marital stress point. Or you may have never worked through the stress that arose when your first child became three months old. Plus, parenting a preschooler is stressful in itself. Many parents say that parenting preschoolers is as stressful as parenting teenagers.

The stress and intensity of parenting a preschooler is the reason why your adult relationships are so important. You need supportive adults around you. You need strong friendships, even if you don't have a lot of time to spend with those friends. Your adult relationships can make your life as a parent much easier and also make your life more personally meaningful.

Time for Yourself

As a parent, it's easy to focus on your everyday life and neglect adult relationships. (After all, your child needs your time and energy.) And if you're also working outside the home, you may think you cannot add one more commitment to your already crammed schedule. Remember that you don't need to invest a lot of time in an adult relationship, but it is important to invest *some* time. If you're struggling to connect with other adults, try one of these ideas:

1. Make it a priority to connect on a regular basis with an adult whose company you especially enjoy. For example, get together once a month for tea or coffee. Or make it a point to talk on the phone—or send each other e-mail messages. Some parents even try to invite a friend over for dinner once a month (or once every couple of months) to keep the relationship going and as a chance for other family members to get to know your adult friends.

2. Attend a block party or neighborhood gathering to meet and get to know some of your neighbors. If you're not sure when people in your neighborhood get together, contact your local city or county government to find out if your neighborhood commemorates National Night Out (which is the first Tuesday evening in August each year).

Otherwise, make it a point to introduce yourself to your neighbors when you see them out and about.

3. Reevaluate and renegotiate your relationships with extended family members. Which individuals are most supportive of you as a parent? Spend more time with those people. What do you need from extended family members? Speak up! Let those people know the relationship is important to you and ask for the attention or help you need.

4. Be honest about important relationships that aren't working. Parents who have joint custody and have a poor or contentious relationship with their former spouse may have a difficult time bringing out the best in their preschoolers. The Visalia YMCA in Visalia, California, set up the Y Safe Exchange Program for court-ordered exchanges

---

BONUS IDEA

Connect with an Old Friend

Remember your best friend from high school? College? Your childhood neighborhood? Are you still in touch? If not, try to connect with your old best friend. You may be surprised that the two of you still connect in a deep and enriching way. For example, one parent of a preschooler called up her old friend across the country to touch base. Not only did they talk about old times but they also discovered they were both parents of preschoolers. A year later, they were getting together, and two friendships were formed: one between the adults and another between the preschoolers.

---

between parents with joint custody. Program leaders help parents work through their relationship and create goals that benefit everyone in the family. Look for programs and resources in your area or seek counseling if you have a critical adult relationship that needs help.

5. Pay attention to the adults around you. You may not talk to most of them, but you probably see many of the same adults on a regular basis as you take your child to preschool, go to work, or walk to the library. Periodically strike up a conversation with one of these adults. Even if you don't form a lasting friendship, it can be nice to feel like you have allies throughout your day.

Boredom

Your preschooler wants you to read aloud the same book over and over. Your child keeps shouting "watch me" as she does the same thing over and over at the playground. Your child plays the same music again and again on his music player. When you try to introduce something new to do with your child, or change a story slightly, your child resists.

Because of the way children learn (through repetition and practice), some aspects of parenting can get boring. Children do the same thing over and over—things that you could master in a few minutes. The daily routines that help your child thrive can soon make you yawn.

That's okay. Feelings of boredom signal that you need as much stimulation as your child. The trick, however, is to balance your child's needs with your own. Some parents set aside a regular time for themselves to take a class or learn a new hobby. Two-parent families can take turns putting the children to bed each evening so that one parent has a free evening to pursue other interests. A single parent can link up with another single parent to take turns having a weekend afternoon away.

If it's difficult to get some time alone, be creative with your time. Dr. Stanley Greenspan, an expert in child development, recommends in his book *Playground Politics* (Reading, MA: Addison-Wesley, 1993) setting aside 30 minutes a day for "floor time" where you get down on the floor with your child and play with your child on his terms. "The goal, no matter where you are or what you are doing, is to follow your child's lead and tune in to whatever interests your child," he says. These 30 minutes not only empower your child but also feed your child the undivided attention he craves. The childlike activity can be a welcome distraction from your everyday responsibilities. Once you start giving your child a daily 30-minute floor time, your child will be less clingy and let you follow some of your own interests—even if you're in the same room together.

Time for Yourself

In our society, we're quick to dismiss negative feelings that we believe aren't productive. Yet feeling bored signals that something needs to change. If you begin to make that change, both you and your child will benefit. Try these ideas:

1. As your preschooler becomes more independent, it's easy to take a backseat in the relationship and do only the required tasks, such as getting your child up in the morning, getting her dressed, feeding her, and so on.

Parenting becomes boring when your role becomes a list of daily tasks without much of a relationship. Be more intentional about connecting with your child, even though children tend to be quite self-absorbed at this age. When she is immersed in a topic (such as trucks or dinosaurs), play along and ask questions. When you become more engaged with your child, your child will become more engaged with you. Gradually, she will become less self-absorbed and more spontaneous in your relationship.

2. Be intentional about getting some adult interaction. Even if you work full time and don't see your child often, it's easy to get focused on getting your work done and not having enough conversations with other adults about topics you find stimulating. Connect with other adults around you and begin going deeper with adult relationships.

3. Ask other parents of preschoolers what they do when they get bored with parenting. (If a parent judges you and says he or she never gets bored, go find another parent who's more honest.) Parenting doesn't always go smoothly, and many parents have creative ideas on how to beat the boredom blues.

4. Take a break from parenting. Get a baby-sitter. Don't fill up your time away from your child with your to-do list. Take a long walk. Get a massage. Do something that slows you down and nurtures you rather than fills up more of your time.

5. Do something new and focused. Take a one-time class on a subject you've always found fascinating, such as floral design, Chinese cooking, a computer or photography class, basic home or car repair, or an art class. Ask for a catalog of one-session classes from your local community education department. Don't overlook free and inexpensive activities, such as joining a book discussion group or volunteering at an animal shelter.

Busyness

Life is full and runs at a fast pace when you're a parent. Not only do you need to care for your child, but you also have a home to care for, friendships to nurture, extended family to remain connected to, other family members to care for (if you have a family bigger than the two of you), and perhaps a job or volunteer commitment. Your days are often booked from early morning to evening—even if your calendar looks empty.

To help families with busyness, the organization Putting Family First suggests many ways to slow down and help parents and children connect in more meaningful ways. Their Web site (www.puttingfamilyfirst.org) raises awareness and includes practical ideas on how to find balance in our overscheduled lives.

Putting the brakes on family busyness often helps you think of ways to cut down on the craziness in your personal life. When one aspect of your life is chaotic, it's often difficult not to have that craziness spill into all aspects of your life. Slowing down all parts of your life and doing what's most important will help your life seem not so frazzled and frayed.

Time for Yourself

It may be tempting to control your schedule when you get busy, but that will only backfire in the long run. Life is all about give and take, so try these ideas to help keep busyness from getting you down:

1. Focus on what's important. Many adults sideline a number of activities during the parenting years because having a family and raising children well is a major focus. Be careful, though, not to cut out too much so that you lose yourself. Keep a piece that's uniquely yours and gets you excited.

2. Schedule time away on a regular basis on your calendar. Some parents take an afternoon alone once a month to reenergize themselves and get away from everything. Working parents sometimes take a lunch break once a week where they pack a lunch from home and take a walk before eating alone in a quiet place.

3. Protect your schedule around busy times of the

year, such as holidays, family members' birthdays, school-year starts (if you have older children), and conferences (if you work). Refuse to add anything to the calendar a few days before and a few days after so that you have some downtime before and after a busy time.

BONUS IDEA

Shut Out the World for a Day

On one day when all family members are home, turn off the phone, refuse to answer the door, and clear the calendar of all commitments. (This works best if you can plan a day with no school or work scheduled.) Have your goal be to spend time together in enriching ways. Play games together. Set up a tent in your home. Have a picnic lunch on the floor. Read books together. The idea is to have a family-focused day that helps you all to connect to each other even more.

---

4. Occasionally analyze your activities to see if they bring out the best in you and other family members. Make changes to give yourself (and your family) new energy. Just because your child has always attended the same child care doesn't mean you shouldn't switch if the center has changed and your child is unhappy. (Yes, you want to keep your child's life consistent, but you don't want to emphasize consistency over quality and happiness.) Sometimes making a change means that your life will become busier in the short term, but it may improve greatly in the long run.

5. Be intentional about how you spend your time relaxing. It's often tempting at the end of a busy day to plop on the couch, watch TV, and eat ice cream. Once in a while, that's not a bad activity, but if it's a daily habit, it's not good. Do other activities to unwind. Take a bike ride. Take a long shower or a bath. Meditate. Read a book. If a novel seems daunting, read *The World's Shortest Stories,* edited by Steve Moss (Philadelphia: Running Press, 1998). Each story is only 55 words long.

Finances

Each year since 1960, the U.S. Department of Agriculture (USDA) has estimated how much it costs to raise a child from birth through age 17. When the figures ($269,520.00 for the highest earners in 2004) are released every year, parents groan and don't know how they can do it. Raising a child is expensive. Forty-one percent of parents say that financial pressures make parenting difficult.

If you take a closer look at the USDA study, it becomes clear that raising a child doesn't cost the same amount for every family. In the 2004 study, for families making less than $41,700 (before taxes), it cost about $7,210 a year to raise a preschooler (or $134,370 from birth to age 17). But families earning more than $70,200 a year (before taxes) found it cost more than double that figure ($14,960 a year to raise a 3- to 5-year-old). Manitoba Agriculture, Food and Rural Initiatives has published a fact sheet estimating that it costs between $9,000 and $10,000 (Canadian dollars) per year to raise a child in that province.

All families—no matter where they live or what their income levels—have ups and downs with finances. "Every family is financially vulnerable to tough times," suggests parenting author Melinda Blau. "How you handle challenges sends messages to your child about responsibility, self-worth, and security."

Time for Yourself

Money management can become just as complicated as parenting. You're constantly bombarded with ideas on how to use your money as a parent (from wills, to saving for college, to paying the bills, to taking out life insurance policies). Try a few of these ideas to make sense of the money madness:

1. Work from a budget. If you've never budgeted before, begin tracking your expenses to see how money moves in and out of your family. (You'll often be surprised.) Financial management works easier when you can create a financial plan.

2. Don't assume you have to buy everything new— or that your child needs to have a lot of toys. Many parents shop second-hand stores for clothes and other items (except for a car seat—always buy that new to ensure that it hasn't been in an accident). Other parents create toy swaps with other parents.

3. Don't spend more than you have. If you have trouble doing this, use only cash, not credit cards and checks.

4. As a parent, it's wise to create a will, if you don't have one already. Although you may not having anything for anyone to inherit, you do want to have a legal document that says who will look after your children if some-

Monitor Your Financial Stress Levels

Money magazine calls the years of parenting the "pressure cooker years" since parents are under extreme financial stress. According to *Money* magazine, parents whose children are living with them have the highest credit-card balances and spend more money on food and entertainment than any other age group. Of course it's important to watch your finances carefully and make wise decisions about money, but try not to let your concerns turn into intense stress. You might find it helpful to balance your worries with plenty of low-cost efforts to relieve stress. When you feel your blood pressure rising because of finances, take time out to breathe deeply, stroll in the sunshine, or chat with friends.

thing happens to you. A life insurance policy—even a small one—may also give you peace of mind.

5. What's your vision about money and how you use it? Nathan Dungan, author of *Prodigal Sons & Material Girls: How Not to Be Your Child's ATM* (New York: Wiley, 2003), has created a share-save-spend model to help you think about how you use your money to share with others, to save, and to spend. Visit www.sharesavespend.com for more ideas.

Guilt

Most days go well, but there are some days when . . .

You don't spend enough time with your child. Your
home is a mess. Your friends are mad at you because you
never have time to be with them. Your parents want more
of you. You aren't happy about the quality of work you've
been doing lately. Everybody wants a bigger piece of you,
and you don't feel like you have anything left. (Plus, what
about what *you* want?)

All parents feel overextended at times, and all parents
feel guilty. It's hard to juggle 50 responsibilities when the
typical human being drops a ball while trying to juggle
three or four.

Ann Pleschette Murphy, author of *The Seven Stages
of Motherhood* (New York: Alfred A. Knopf, 2004), says
that parenting when your children are preschoolers is
the time when most guilt arises. She contends it's because
parents try to do it all and have unrealistic expectations
about what they really can do. She suggests examining
your expectations (and reexamining them often) to ensure that you're not doing too much and doing things
you don't want to do (but feel obligated to do). The best
way to banish guilt is not to be guilty. Create a life that
is meaningful and rewarding to both you and your child,
and you can say good-bye to guilt.

Time for Yourself

Feeling guilty once in a while is normal, but if you're
feeling guilty a lot, something needs to change. Try some
of these ideas to deal with guilty feelings:

If you're not used to treating yourself well, you will most likely feel guilty when you indulge in something wonderful the first time. That's okay. If you can't imagine getting a massage because it's too indulgent and you would feel guilty because other parents don't have the opportunity to get a massage, that's exactly when you need to get one. Pamper yourself once in a while. Enjoy it. Then don't put the pleasure off too long before you do it again.

1. Avoid the comparison game. Just because another parent is doing it all (or doing more than you) doesn't mean you need to compete. Relax. Be yourself. Compare yourself only to your vision of and hopes for your family, not to what others are doing.

2. Are your feelings of guilt valid? Sometimes you might feel guilty because you need to make a change. One parent felt guilty for working full time and being away from her child. Then she felt guilty when she tried being a stay-at-home mom. When she began working part-time, she realized that was what worked best for her, and the guilty feelings eased.

3. Keep away from people who make you feel guilty. Sometimes an individual can cause you to feel guilty by pointing out how you're not being a good parent. Do what's best for you and your child. For some families, that means having a working parent. For others families, it means having a stay-at-home parent. One way isn't better than the other (even though some people have strong opinions about this). Parent in the way that works best for you. Take care of yourself in the way that works for you, and stay away from the naysayers.

4. Change your expectations and commitments. If you're a runner who competes in 10 races a year, maybe you need to cut back to one or two a year. When you cut back on things, remember that there will be other years when you will have more time. Parenting young children is a labor-intensive time, but the time demands often ease when children start elementary school.

5. Learn more about child development. It's easy to feel guilty as a parent if you don't know that healthy children develop at different rates. *Caring for Your Baby and Young Child: Birth to Age 5* by the American Academy of Pediatrics (New York: Bantam Books, 2004) gives helpful, authoritative advice on what's normal development for children at each age. It shows that some children may develop verbal skills earlier but lag in gross motor skills (walking, running, and climbing). Others develop in the opposite way, and all these children are developing normally—and on time.

Isolation

You're a single parent, and you feel all alone. You're married, and you feel like a single parent. You're parenting an adopted child of another race, and other people stare at you and your child. You wish you didn't feel so alone.

From time to time, all parents feel isolated and alone.

They wish others understood them better and that they had more support.

It's time to start building your network of support.

You don't have to be an extrovert to connect with other people. Introduce yourself to other parents who take their preschoolers to the playground or park. Strike up a conversation with another parent in the waiting room for the pediatrician. Get to know the parents of your child's friends. If your community has an asset-building initiative, get involved. (Go to www.search-institute.org/communities/partner.html to find a community in your area.)

Little by little, expand your network of support and deepen the relationships that you do have. You'll feel less alone.

BONUS IDEA

Create an E-Mail Network of Support

Many parents find that it's difficult to get together since everyone has busy schedules. One mom decided to stay in touch with other moms by asking for their e-mail addresses. Occasionally, she dropped them a line to check in. She quickly found that other parents wanted to connect but also struggled with how to do this consistently in person. One mom always sent e-mail in the middle of the night. One was on her computer early in the morning, while another found time for e-mail around midnight.

Time for Yourself

Parenting a preschooler can sometimes feel like living in a fish bowl. You spend all of your time providing the ideal environment for your child and you end up isolating yourself in the process. (Don't panic; that's normal.) To feel less isolated, try these ideas:

1. Look for an interesting program to attend with your child where you will meet other families with preschoolers. Your local YMCA, ECFE (Early Childhood Family Education), and community education organizations often offer classes and programs. Faith communities and health clubs sometimes provide free child care for adults attending classes or events.

2. When your child takes an interest in another child at preschool or a child-care center, ask the parent for the family's phone number. Arrange a playdate, and get to know the parent as well.

3. If your child is involved in a preschool, child-care center, or community program, ask if there's a parent group (or one that could be created). Often programs have a parent advisory group where you can meet other parents.

4. Reconnect with old friends. Although your best friend may live across the country, he or she may also be a parent and be interested in connecting again. Some adults have found old friends and created family friends where families take turns visiting each other. (The children then also become friends.) Others have kept in touch via the phone, instant and text-messaging, e-mail, or mail.

5. If you enjoy cooking, invite another family with a preschooler over for dinner once a month. As the children play, you can get to know the parent(s) better. Eating together in the home often helps relationships to form and become deeper more quickly.

Job Demands

If you are employed, your job adds another layer of complexity to your parenting life. Yes, the job provides financial resources (and sometimes other benefits), but it also takes up more of your time and energy.

The majority of parents work outside the home, and a lot of them enjoy their work—and their parenting. Yet, a Search Institute/YMCA of the USA poll of 1,005 parents revealed that half of parents surveyed say that job demands make parenting difficult. Job demands were the number one stressor among these parents.

Pay close attention to how your job affects your family and how your family affects your job. Some jobs require a lot of overtime or extra work that needs to be taken home and finished after hours. Some jobs are more open to the give-and-take of families, understanding that sometimes a job requires more of your time during certain times of the year while your family requires more of your time during other parts of the year.

As an employee, advocate for a working situation that benefits you, your family, and your employer. (Everyone likes a win-win situation.) Talk with other working parents to see what works for them. Some parents have created job-share positions. Others have created more flexibility by working part of the time in the office and part of the time at home.

Time for Yourself

Balancing work and family is an ongoing challenge for parents, but you can make it easier by trying a few of these ideas:

1. Learn as much as you can about your company's work-family policies. Can you take sick time (or vacation time) to care for a sick child? Does your company have a flexible-benefits plan that allows you to use pre-tax dollars for child-care expenses? If your child care closes, can you bring your child to work—or work from home?

2. Get everyone in your family to pitch in with household chores so that one working parent isn't juggling two big jobs: the one at the office and the responsibilities at

---

BONUS IDEA

Create a Colorful Family Calendar

Color code your family calendar so that you and your child can clearly see which days you spend together as a family and which days you're separated because of work. For example, color the days you're together yellow and all the separated days green. Some parents even color code their work days as half green and half yellow to show that they get to spend part of their day with their child. To highlight time for yourself, place a box around a certain timeframe, and save that time for you.

home. It's also problematic if a stay-at-home parent bears all responsibility for housework and parenting. If you have a partner, divide family responsibilities so that one partner isn't overwhelmed.

3. If your job requires travel, create travel boundaries so that traveling doesn't get out of hand. Some parents (along with their employers) agree on one trip per month while seeking other alternatives, such as conference calls, finding a coworker who can travel instead, creating shorter trips, and consolidating two trips into one. When you do travel, call your child on the phone and bring back a small gift when you return.

4. Decorate your office (if company policy allows you to) with your child's drawings and photographs. Occasionally take your child to the office (even if it's after hours) so that she knows where you work and sees how you've surrounded yourself with pictures of her.

5. Add some spice to your commute by going home from work by a different route. As a working parent, you can have such a tight schedule that some of your daily routines can become repetitious and mind numbing.

Letting Go

Parenting is like learning how to dance. You step forward to get to know your child more. You step back to let your child become more independent. The dance of parenting involves stepping forward (bonding and attaching) and stepping back (letting go).

The preschool years may be the first time you've become aware of needing to let go. As your preschooler grows and changes, it's obvious that you've lost that baby you adored so much and now have this energetic child who may seem somewhat foreign. That's normal. Part of parenting is about feeling nostalgic for the past and letting it go while embracing what's happening right before your eyes.

Letting go also is about controlling your child less, which isn't easy to do when your child misbehaves. Yes, you need to set boundaries and enforce them, but you cannot control how your child will feel or act. What's important is focusing on how *you* act and to keep working with your child to influence her to act in more acceptable ways.

Time for Yourself

Our society emphasizes acquiring and holding onto things rather than letting them go. Relationships, however, don't work that way. Build a positive relationship with yourself (and your child) by learning to let go of a variety of things. Try these ideas:

1. Since parenting is one of your priorities, learn to let go of some other things. Retired professional baseball player Harmon Killebrew remembers how his father used to play with him and his brother in the yard and his mother would come out and complain that they were tearing up the grass. Harmon remembers his dad saying: "We're not raising grass; we're raising boys."

2. Pay attention to where you carry stress in your body. Do you drive with too firm a grip on the steering wheel? Do your shoulders or neck tighten when life is stressful? Does your·lower back get sore? Take time each day to relax your body—and your muscles.

Take Time to Play

Do something fun every day, even if it's only for a few moments. "The responsibility of parenthood often strips people's lives of fun and lightness," says Jeanne Bassis, founder of PlayReflections. "But you can learn a lot from your children about living in the moment, letting go of everyday stresses, and forgetting about what other people think."

3. Which gives you more energy: juggling multiple tasks simultaneously or focusing on one task at a time? Parenting preschoolers automatically puts you into dealing with multiple tasks and demands. If you thrive more by doing one thing at a time, be more intentional about living that way and cutting down the number of things you do.

4. If you have the tendency to be a perfectionist, be aware that this tendency can lead you to a lot of frustration since parenting is often a messy, less-than-perfect process. Be easy on yourself. See if you can become more flexible in some aspects of your life while using your perfectionism for projects you want to do well.

5. Parenting a preschooler takes a lot of energy, and it's helpful to keep your energy moving. Some parents have found that they need a physical outlet (some type of exercise or sport) to parent well. Others find that they need to release pent-up emotional energy by going off alone sometimes to cry, scream, or vent.

Personal Purpose

As a parent, your life is full and busy. But what is your personal purpose? What makes you jump out of bed in the morning?

"It does not matter what the ultimate goal is—provided it is compelling enough to order a life-time's worth of psychic energy," says Mihaly Csikszentmihalyi, author of *Flow: The Psychology of Optimal Experience* (New York: Harper & Row, 1990). "As long as it provides clear objectives, clear rules for action, and a way to concentrate and become involved, any goal can serve to give meaning to a person's life."

You can find personal purpose in parenting, a job, volunteer work, or hobbies. You can find it in more than one place. What matters is that you believe your life has a purpose and that you're doing everything you can to fulfill that purpose.

Time for Yourself

Personal purpose is one of the Developmental Assets (asset 39: sense of purpose). It's a key aspect of having a strong identity and finding meaning in life. Try some of these ideas to identify and act on your own sense of purpose:

1. Few people identify their personal purpose early in life and then stick with that purpose. Most people find one purpose, follow it for a while, lose a sense of purpose from time to time, and then discover a new purpose. Some people have multiple purposes and emphasize some over others at certain times of their lives. Take time to identify your personal purpose and follow it. But also be patient with yourself when you become rudderless.

2. Most people know that a personal purpose requires enthusiasm (or passion) and skill. Which interests do you have that are undeveloped? How can you build your skill level? If you've lost your passion for something, is it because you need a break or you need to go in a new direction? Stay-at-home parents who plan to return to work someday may find it especially rewarding to seek experiences that prepare them for future career goals.

3. If you've lost your sense of purpose, talk with people who know you well and ask for their opinions. What do they think is your sense of purpose? Also go back and list accomplishments you were most proud of in the past. Is your sense of purpose buried somewhere in that list?

4. Be intentional about your purpose as a parent. Do you want to be an asset-building parent? If so, how do

BONUS IDEA

A Helpful Book

What Color Is Your Parachute? is written and updated every year by Richard Nelson Bolles and Mark Emery Bolles (Berkeley, CA: Ten Speed Press). This book gives helpful tips on how to find your passion and live the life you want. Although the major focus is on careers, the book contains helpful guides on identifying your interests.

you define asset-building parenting? How can you bring out the best in your child? Although your parenting will change somewhat as your child grows, you can be intentional about your overall parenting vision and goals.

5. In our task-oriented society, it's easy to overlook and undervalue a personal purpose that emphasizes relationships and people skills. When reflecting on your personal purpose, also consider your skills of empathy, listening, mediating, service, problem solving, humor, decision making, motivating others, planning, meeting new people, and getting people to open up and talk about personal issues.

Reenergizing Yourself

When was the last time you did something for yourself? As a parent, it's easy to put your child first and yourself last. That means on some days you discover that there aren't any leftover moments for you, and if you don't take time for yourself, you can eventually lose yourself.

As an asset-building parent, it's as essential to nurture your own assets as it is to build assets for your child. The first step to doing that is to take time for yourself and to choose activities that reenergize you, rather than turning your mind and body to mush.

Instead of clicking on the TV late at night or grabbing another bowl of popcorn, think about what you used to do that opened you up. Did you ever play a musical instrument? Sing? Skate? Jog? Grow African violets? Read books? Laugh with a friend over the phone?

The best time to reenergize yourself is *before* you're stressed and burned out. When you're energized about life in general, you're more likely to have the energy and wits to parent your child well.

Time for Yourself

Is it possible to burn out from parenting by the time your child turns three? Yes. It happens to almost all parents, and it can happen many times during your years of parenting. Prevent parenting burnout by taking time for yourself:

1. If your personal and family calendars fill up fast, set times to recharge yourself. (Actually set a date on your calendar.) When you're intentional about making time for yourself, you're more apt to take it.

2. Examine your personal habits and routines. Which energize you? Which drain you? Which things do you do as a way to cope? What one change would energize you?

3. Ask other parents how they take time for themselves. Not only may you discover new ideas, but you'll open up interesting conversations about the topic.

BONUS IDEA

Recharge Yourself with Humor

Read compilation books of cartoons, such as *Calvin and Hobbes* by Bill Watterson or *For Better or for Worse* by Lynn Johnston, to help you laugh more about the ups and downs of parenting.

---

4. Adapt one of your relaxing activities to make it more indulgent. For example, instead of reading a novel, rent an audio novel from the library.

5. Do nothing. Sometimes the best way to recharge your spirit is to stop for a while and slow down your schedule until you have more energy and enthusiasm.

Sleep Deprivation

Everybody knows about parental sleep deprivation when your child is a newborn, but you'll probably be surprised that you'll have periods of sleep deprivation when your child is a preschooler (and then again when your child becomes a teenager). Since parenting is a 24-hour, seven-day-a-week position, you'll never know when you're needed in the middle of the night—and for multiple nights.

Preschoolers get sick. They may panic when they get sick, and they often don't sleep. Preschoolers also are prone to night terrors and nightmares, and they can wake you up in the middle of the night with screams of terror. All this is normal, and all this can lead to sleep deprivation. (Plus, you never know when *you'll* get sick.)

Some parents can hobble along fairly well with sleep deprivation; others can't. Discern how well you deal with sleep deprivation, but be realistic. You don't want to endanger yourself, your child, or anybody else if you're a walking zombie.

Nap (Yes, Again) When Your Child Naps

Experts say that it's smart for parents of newborns to nap when their babies nap so that they can catch up on a few winks themselves. Even though you now have a preschooler, this is still a wise thing to do during periods when your child may be waking you up a lot in the middle of the night and you're exhausted. Take good care of yourself, and you'll be better able to take good care of your child.

Time for Yourself

The news often reports that we're a sleep-deprived society, but parents can quickly become even more sleep-deprived than other adults. Try some of these ideas to keep your sanity (and your health) when you're exhausted:

1. When your child wakes consistently in the night (because of sickness, night terrors, or nightmares), cut back on your other obligations. Let the dishes sit in the sink longer than usual. Let your home be more messy than usual. Reschedule appointments to a date when (hopefully) you're not so tired. As you pull out of your sleep-deprived state, slowly catch up on the tasks you let slide.

2. Eat healthy foods and avoid a lot of sugary and caffeinated foods. When you're tired, it's tempting to take caffeine to wake you up and to eat sugary foods to get your blood sugar up. This only gives you short-term benefits and can make it harder for you to fall asleep when you do want to sleep.

3. Try to create more time for short naps and try to get to bed earlier. Make sleep a higher priority than usual—until you're not so exhausted.

4. Closely monitor your health when you're sleep deprived. Some people get headaches when they're tired. Others get sick. Avoid treating your other symptoms (such as taking pain killers to deal with headaches) when what you really need is more sleep.

5. Ask for help. Enlist the help of an older sibling, an extended family member, or a baby-sitter to spend time with your preschooler while you get some much-needed sleep. Other people will often be happy to help. Maybe an extended family member will even take your child overnight (as long as this person knows that your child could wake up) so that you can get one full night of sleep.

Stress

As a parent juggling numerous responsibilities, you'll often run into stress. You never know when your child will have an emotional outburst. You never know when life will fling an upsetting situation your way. All you know is that stress strikes, sometimes when you least expect it.

The truth about parenting preschoolers is that it is often exhausting. Preschoolers have boundless energy, and they're developing so quickly that it can feel chaotic trying to parent them. Parenting a preschooler can be downright stressful.

The more you know what stresses you (and what stresses you might not stress someone else), the more you can get the upper hand. Breathe deeply. Exercise or go for a brisk walk. Take a short break, even if it's only to step out of the room for a few seconds. You and your child will both benefit.

BONUS IDEA

Indulge Yourself

The biggest stress busters are the ones that feel self-indulgent. What do you truly enjoy doing? What have you loved doing in the past that you might not have done recently? Anything on your list of "I-could-never-do-that" that's truly good for you is worth pursuing.

Time for Yourself

Stress is so common that it's easy to take it for granted. As a parent, however, your stress levels affect your child. Try these ideas to handle stress more effectively:

1. Create buffer zones in your schedule. Running from one activity to the next only adds stress to your day. Add more time for transitions so that you're not running yourself ragged.

2. Monitor yourself to ensure that you're handling stress well. If you're under serious stress, you're more likely to pull away from people, get sick more than usual, have trouble sleeping, struggle to concentrate, fear making decisions, feel trapped, and be frequently irritated. Seek help from your doctor or another professional if stress is getting the best of you.

3. If you feel stressed often, track your emotions during the day (or on a weekly calendar). What patterns do you see? Then make changes so that you're less stressed.

4. Keep your eyes open for the little stressors that can sneak up on you. Sitting too long in one position can stress your muscles and create aches and pains. Be aware of the minor irritating behaviors that your child does that can build up and cause you to explode if you don't defuse the tension.

5. Play hooky when you can. Can you occasionally take a longer lunch break? Or take a few hours off to go to the movies? Sleep in a bit later one morning. Go fishing. Put on dance music that you like and dance with your child on the kitchen floor. Hire a neighborhood teenager to run your errands so that you can relax when you get a baby-sitter.

Taking Breaks from Parenting

With tight budgets, crammed schedules, and a concern for your child's safety, you can end up spending all of your time with your child and never taking a break. Yet, short times away from your child not only are a good idea—they are a necessity.

"If you feel overwhelmed at times, don't panic," says Dr. Louise Hart, author of *The Winning Family: Increasing Self-Esteem in Your Children and Yourself* (Berkeley, CA: Celestial Arts, 1993). "Sometimes what you need is to get away from the kids for a while—walk in the woods, visit a friend, go dancing—to help you relax and regain perspective."

Even if you don't feel overwhelmed, taking an occasional break can help clear your mind and give you a better, more realistic outlook about life overall. (We take breaks from everything else, so why can't we give ourselves a break from parenting from time to time?) Hire a baby-sitter. Make an exchange with another parent where one hangs out with the kids while the other does something else to rejuvenate himself or herself. Take turns giving each other breaks.

Time for Yourself

Find some time for yourself by giving yourself a breather from your child. Try some of these ideas:

1. Figure out a way to take regular breaks. If you have a parenting partner, arrange to meet for a meal or a walk (just the two of you) on a regular basis. If you're a single parent, look for a preschool program in your community or congregation. Some offer inexpensive programs with the idea of giving parents a break and children something fascinating to do.

2. Take a short mental break. Close your eyes. Breathe deeply. Relax your muscles. You don't have to always leave your child to get away.

3. If you're a single parent and would like an inexpensive getaway, visit www.SingleParentTravel.net. This Web site includes a monthly newsletter with tips and destination suggestions. If you're married, get away for a weekend with your spouse through Marriage Encounter. Call 800-828-3351 or visit www.marriage-encounter.org.

4. Make sure you take regular breaks to eat and to care for yourself. Some parents end up skipping meals because getting the kids fed can be chaotic and stressful at times. If that happens, take time to eat afterward.

5. Plan for a longer getaway. Go away for an entire day, a weekend, or a short week. Make arrangements for someone to care for your child while you go off. Maybe a friend owns a cabin that you can use for a few days. Rent a hotel room. Arrange a house swap with another parent. Visit another city that you've always wanted to see.

Unsolicited Advice

"Isn't she too old for that?" "You shouldn't spoil him like that." "When I was a parent, we *never* did that."

Unsolicited advice. It can come from anywhere: a stranger, an in-law, a neighbor, even a good friend. If the advice is genuinely helpful or isn't a big deal, it will roll off your shoulders. But if it's given with emotion (and the expectation that you *should* follow it), then it's harder to handle.

Asset builders want the best for children, and sometimes people can have opposing viewpoints about parenting preschoolers. In fact, when it comes to unsolicited advice, you usually find that some people have strong opinions about certain parenting matters.

Remember: When someone has a strong opinion, it's their issue, not yours. (Don't you think it's odd that this person wants *you* to parent *your child* in *her* or *his* way?) Maybe this person has issues with control (which is why you feel unsettled and controlled). Maybe this person means well but lacks some tact.

You're your child's parent. People can give their advice, but only you can decide whether you want to follow it.

BONUS IDEA

Stand Up for Yourself—Carefully

Some people don't get the hint when you subtly tell them that you can parent your child in your own way. When that happens, sometimes you need to be more direct, but you can do so carefully and with gentleness. The next time "that someone" gives you more unsolicited advice, say, "I know you're concerned about my child, but I am (name your child)'s parent. I have decided to (name what you're disagreeing about)." Adults can disagree. As an adult with integrity, you can disagree in ways that show respect for differing opinions.

Time for Yourself

The best advice is the advice you ask for, but unfortunately, that's not always how advice comes. When people give you unsolicited advice (particularly bad advice), try some of these ideas:

1. Keep your sense of humor. If someone is judging (for example, pointing out that your child isn't eating anything), make a comment about your child acting in the opposite way. For example, "You should have seen her yesterday. She ate four helpings of macaroni and cheese. No wonder she's not hungry today." Then laugh and change the subject.

2. Thank the person for the advice (even if it's ludicrous) and change the subject. For example, say, "Thanks for the tip. I'll think about it." Then talk about something else.

3. If you're rattled by the advice (even if the advice isn't good), take some time to sort through the reason the comment bothered you. Is it about an aspect of parenting that you feel unsure about? Is it something you already wish you were doing differently? Is it because you're seeing a side of the person you've never seen before? Is it because you're tired? Is it because the person is trying to manipulate you?

4. If the same person continues to hound you and will not respect the fact that *you're* the parent (and this person is *not*), keep away from this person. If you have to interact with this person (perhaps because he or she is related to you), avoid the topic of parenting. Always be ready with a long list of topics the other person enjoys talking about. (Diversion works as well with adults as it does with children.)

5. Focus on the positive aspect of your conversation. For example, some people feel a bond with parents of young children because they miss having (or seeing) children at that age. Ask: What did you enjoy about this age group? Sometimes the person will back down and begin to talk about himself or herself instead.

PART 3

*Taking Care
of Your Child*

Bathing

You can't get them in the bathtub. Then once they're in, you can't get them out. Young children can be notorious for resisting baths. They run away. They hide. They sometimes kick and scream. That's because many children know that when bath time comes, bedtime is next, and they're not ready to end the day.

Fortunately, kids won't resist baths all the time. Bath times typically become battle times when children turn 3½—and when they're feeling powerless. They'll resist and object to assert themselves, which is a good thing for them, but not an easy thing for adults.

Making bath time another playtime often goes a long way in relieving the bath-time blues. Some children enjoy a short game of chase before getting in the tub. Others like to choose three plastic toys to bathe with them. Still others enjoy hearing a good book that you read while sitting close by.

SPOTLIGHT ON ASSETS

Asset 17: Play and Creative Activities

Bath time is more than just getting children clean. Make bath time a creative time when your preschooler can stretch his imagination. Encourage your child to tell stories of animals floating on boats and people who live under the sea. When bath time becomes another playtime, preschoolers are more apt to look forward to this part of your routine.

Create a Water Wonder

Freeze a small plastic toy in a paper cup filled with water. Tear away the cup after the water freezes, and let your child enjoy playing with the toy as the glacier melts in the tub. (You might also add food coloring to the water before you freeze it.) Or dump a tray of ice cubes into the tub and see what your child does.

Whatever you do, aim to make bath time fun instead of a power struggle. Then maybe your child won't be the only one who doesn't want bath time to end!

Time Together

Sometimes it's the ordinary times that become the most memorable. Make the most of your child's bathtub time by trying some of these ideas:

1. If your child resists having a bath, announce that you're a camel (or an elephant, or a train). Get down on all fours and invite your child to ride you to the bathroom.

2. If you're tired, kick off your shoes and stick your bare feet in the tub next to your child. Invite your child to scrub your feet or "paint" your legs with soap. As you relax, open yourself up to the bath-time world of your child.

3. Pull out the bubble solution and the bubble wand that you usually use outside and use it in the bathtub.

4. Sing silly bathtub songs to your child with *Take Me*

Out of the Bathtub and Other Silly Dilly Songs by Alan Katz (New York: Margaret K. McElderry Books, 2001).

5. Preschoolers love to play with toys in the bathtub, but sometimes they can make a mess, splashing water over the edge of the tub. Try offering a small plastic step stool to use as a "table" in the tub, and your child will have a safe place to play without drenching the bathroom floor.

Bed-wetting

If your preschooler wets the bed, you're not alone. Most preschoolers wet the bed—even after they've been toilet trained. In fact, after your child has been toilet trained during the day, it may take up to two years (or even longer) before she will stay consistently dry through the night. Young preschoolers can wet the bed two to three times a week, and most children don't stop wetting the bed until around age 5, says the American Academy of Pediatrics.

Bed-wetting is a physical situation (a young child's bladder isn't large enough to hold a full night of urine), not a behavior issue. When your preschooler wets the bed, don't make a big deal of it. Explain that bed-wetting happens to all preschoolers. It's all part of growing up.

Even if your child stays dry at night for many days or weeks, bed-wetting can occur again. If that happens, treat it as something natural. If it happens more than once, put your child back into training pants (during bedtimes only) and monitor how your child does.

Some children (mainly boys) can continue to wet the bed past the age of 5. This affects 1 out of every 10 children, so it's more common than you may think. Some preschoolers have unusually small bladders, so they continue to wet the bed every night until age 4 or 5.

Keep your pediatrician informed about bed-wetting, particularly if your child complains of pain or burning while urinating—or if you intuitively feel something is wrong. It's always best to check to ensure that your child is developmentally on track. It will bring you peace of mind, which is always a plus in parenting.

Time Together

Children learn a lot about themselves by the way you react when they wet the bed. Try these ideas to ensure that you're not overreacting to bed-wetting.

1. Protect the mattress on your child's bed. Use stain-resistant spray and consider placing a zippered, plastic mattress cover over the mattress. Check it twice a year to ensure that the mattress cover hasn't ripped.

SPOTLIGHT ON ASSETS

Asset 32: Planning and Decision Making

Include your child in making up the bed the morning after she wets the bed. Let her pick which sheets to put on next. Letting children make choices builds their planning and decision-making skills. After you've cleaned up the bed and made it, invite your child to select her favorite stuffed animals and dolls and place them on the bed.

Move Closer to Your Child

Usually it's the parent who has a harder time with bed-wetting than the child. As a parent, you want to help your child, and with bed-wetting (especially if it becomes frequent), you can quickly become frustrated and feel helpless. Adding to the problem is that some preschoolers may seem oblivious to bed-wetting, which may annoy you even more. Instead of getting upset, see yourself as your child's main support. (Your child actually may be as discouraged as you but not show it.) How can you encourage your child or be understanding? Figure out a way to connect with your child in the morning after he wets the bed (even if it's tempting to pull away in irritation). Play a short game together. Sing a song. Dance in the kitchen while you're making breakfast. Do something fun together so bed-wetting doesn't create distance between the two of you.

2. Let your child choose disposable training pants to wear to bed. Explain that being toilet trained during the day comes first and staying dry at night comes later—and your child is right on track. Even if you wish your child would develop sooner in this area, send a clear message of support.

3. Although bed-wetting is normal during the preschool years, consider these ideas so that your child doesn't flood the bed: Have your child cut back on the number of liquids and salty foods at the end of the day. Make bedtime a relaxing time. Some children are sensitive to stress, which can affect their bladder.

4. Keep a calendar. If you think your child has a bed-wetting problem or constantly wets the bed, make note of which days your child is wet in the morning on a calendar. Continue keeping the calendar over a few months—and even years. Typically you'll see your child staying dry a night here and there, which becomes more common (slowly) as they grow older. Celebrate these improvements together.

5. Have your child go to the bathroom before he goes to bed at night. Even if you child doesn't have to go, the sound of running water in the sink may help trigger urination. Making a trip to the bathroom part of your preschooler's bedtime ritual is a good habit that may make a difference over time.

Blankets and Security Items

Don't be surprised if your 3-year-old leaves her blanket behind most of the time and then wants it constantly around age 3½. The preschool years are full of periods of growing up and then moments of clinging to younger stages.

Allow your child to keep his blanket, stuffed animal, or other "transition" item—even if you think your child is too old for it. In fact, most kids are attached to certain items for a long time, and these attachments are healthy. These items bring your child comfort, and they often help

Asset 26: Caring

Talking about the items your child is attached to
(and the ones you were attached to as a child) helps
your child know that you understand how he feels.
Everyone is attached to something, and being attached
to something shows that you have deep emotions.
Encourage your child to treat other children, pets, and
adults in the caring, tender way he treats a beloved
blanket or toy.

your child release tension or feel secure when he is apart
from you.

This is fine until other kids start to tease your child
for being a "baby" when having a certain item. When this
happens, be creative in how you help your child make
the transition to attaching to something else or attaching
to the same item in a new way. Some children can give
up carting around a blanket by carrying a small piece of
it (their mini blanky) in their pocket as a sense of security. Other preschoolers have to bring a blanket with them.
Encourage your child to bring a stuffed animal too, and
then try to relax the attachment by slowly suggesting that
the blanket belongs to the stuffed animal.

If you still have an item you used to carry around
as a child, show it to your preschooler. Talk about how
much you loved this item and how much it comforted
you. If the item is dirty and worn, explain that it got this

way because you loved it and used it so much. Blankets and security items give children a sense of identity. Cherish these items and allow your child to cherish them too.

Time Together

Preschoolers aren't the only ones who carry security items with them. So do many adults. These items may give us courage, remind us of the people we love, or comfort us. Some adults carry a meaningful symbol around with them in their pockets or purses. Do you carry a family photo in your wallet? This is more than feeling proud about your family. It's a symbol of what you have and how important those relationships are to you. When adults need to do something difficult or frightening, they may wear a favorite piece of clothing that makes them feel more courageous—or they may carry a small item, such as a ceramic eagle to remind them to spread their wings wide and not shrivel up.

To help your child with security items, try these ideas:

1. Celebrate how a blanket or some other object helps your child feel. Since preschoolers have a strong imagination, they often give lifelike characteristics to their security object. Ask your child about this, and encourage your child to take good care of his item.

2. Notice the objects other preschoolers are attached to. Ask them questions about their items: Where did you get it? How long have you had it? How does it make you feel? What do you love best about it?

3. If the wear and tear is driving you crazy, find a way to clean the item or repair it instead of replacing it. Adults care much more about how something looks than children do, so don't let your feelings override your child's.

4. If your child will not let go of an item that you feel she has outgrown, figure out another way for her to have it. For example, a baby blanket can be cut into smaller squares and carried as a handkerchief in a pocket.

BONUS IDEA

Help Your Child to Let Go

If you believe your child should let go of a strong attachment, you can do so in a delicate way. One set of preschool parents felt strongly that their daughter ought to give up her pacifier (which she was very attached to). They began by having her take breaks from the pacifier, and encouraged her to pay more attention to other toys and people. When the child was using the pacifier only one hour a week, the parents bought a helium balloon and helped her let go of the balloon (after playing with it) and watch it float away. They said when she felt ready to let go of her pacifier, they would buy another helium balloon, attach the pacifier to it, and say good-bye together. The parents ended up buying three helium balloons at three separate times when their daughter didn't want to let go at the last minute. Finally, she was ready. They tied her pacifier to the balloon, and they all waved good-bye to it together, and the daughter never asked to use the pacifier again.

---

5. Some parents try to replace a well-worn stuffed animal or doll. If you do, don't throw the old one out. Most likely your child will get attached to both of them, and you'll now have two special items to provide comfort instead of one.

Child Care

A significant person in your child's life (besides you) is your child's caregiver. Your child may not see this person every day, but this person helps to mold your child's thinking, decision making, and values.

Unfortunately, many barriers exist to finding and keeping high-quality caregivers. Many parents face high turnover, high demand, high cost, and long waiting lists, and it's not easy to maneuver through these barriers. In addition, each state and province sets different requirements for caregiving. Montana requires child-care centers to have one adult for every eight 3-year-olds. In Florida and Georgia, child-care centers must have one adult for every fifteen 3-year-olds. In Canada, the province of New Brunswick requires one adult for every seven 3-year-olds. In Prince Edward Island and Saskatchewan, the ratio is one adult for every ten 3-year-olds.

Differences between states and provinces are even greater for older children. In Connecticut, Vermont, South Dakota, Montana, and Minnesota, child-care centers must have one adult for every ten children who are age 5. In Florida, child-care centers can have one adult for every 25 children who are five years old. In British Columbia

*Asset 6: Parent Involvement in
Child Care and Education*

Your child will benefit more from child care when you
get involved—and stay involved. Some parents participate through child-care governing boards. Others
help out with special events. Even if there are not formal ways to become involved, you can participate by
touching base with caregivers each day and request-
ing a yearly (or semi-annual) progress report.

and the Yukon Territory, one adult must be present for
every eight 5-year-olds. That ratio is one adult to fifteen
5-year-olds in the province of Nova Scotia.

No matter where you live, you can make child care
work for you. Some parents have found child-care centers that have better staff-child ratios than their state or
provincial minimum requirements. Other parents have
formed child-care groups or co-ops (perhaps 3 to 4 families) in which each adult takes a turn caring for the
children while the other adults are away from their children. Others have found a responsible teenager who
baby-sits regularly for certain families. Some have advo-
cated that their workplace create a child-care room or
center, provide child-care benefits, or offer flexible time-
off policies so parents can take time off to care for a sick
child. Although it's true that some parents have more
access to high-quality child care than others, it's also true

that parents who are creative and resourceful can often find child-care opportunities that work well for them—and their child. Some have a grandparent or extended-family member who is willing to provide child care. Other families have teamed together so that one parent can earn a living providing child care for the other working parents. The possibilities are endless.

CHILD-CARE OPTIONS

Family (In-home) Child Care	**Benefits:** • Tends to be the least expensive. • Tends to provide an atmosphere most like yours at home. **Concerns:** • When a provider becomes ill, there is no back up. • Some states and provinces don't have stringent licensing requirements for in-home child-care facilities.
Child-Care Center	**Benefits:** • Tends to have a more structured and educational approach to child care. • When a provider becomes ill, there are other providers who can fill in. **Concerns:** • Some child-adult ratios can become high (depending on state or provincial requirements). • Some large centers with standardized rules may have less capacity to be flexible about some family preferences.

Educational Child Care (Montessori, Waldorf, etc.)	**Benefits:** • Provides high-quality educational instruction. • Providers may have higher educational levels and less turnover. **Concerns:** • Tends to be the most expensive. • Tends to follow an educational calendar, so they're not in operation as many days as other child-care centers.

Sources (contact for more information): National Association for the Education of Young Children (NAEYC), Washington, D.C., www.naeyc.org; National Association for Family Child Care, Salt Lake City, Utah, www.nafcc.org; National Child Care Association, Washington, D.C., www.nccanet.org; National Network for Child Care, Ames, Iowa, www.nncc.org; Association of Waldorf Schools of North America, Fair Oaks, California, www.awsna.org; The International Montessori Index, Columbia, Maryland, www.montessori.edu.

Time Together

Your child isn't the only one who needs to spend time with his caregiver. It's also essential that you spend quality time with your child's caregiver. The time doesn't need to be extensive, but it does need to count. Try these ideas:

1. Whenever your child starts a new child-care center or you hire a new baby-sitter, try to schedule 30 minutes to 1 hour to stay with your child and the new caregiver on the first day. This gives your child a chance to warm up slowly and get used to the new person.

2. Learn the names of each person who cares for your child. Greet them by name each time you see them. Get

to know them well. By taking an interest in them, they'll
likely take more of an interest in your child.

3. Say what you appreciate about the caregiver, and
be specific. For example, say, "I love the creative crafts
you find" or "You're so patient and loving, especially when
my child is having a hard time." Tensions sometimes exist
between parents and caregivers because both parties are
often stressed, busy, and may have different ideas of how
to raise children well. Begin by assuming the best about
your child-care provider. Take the time to build a relationship with the person. Then when you have disagreements,
such as about discipline, you can talk and work together
rather than get locked into a power struggle.

4. If a family member (or extended family member)
provides child care for you, periodically talk about whether

the arrangement works for everyone—and what could make it better. Be careful not to take advantage of this person since it's easy to expect more of family members than strangers.

5. Finding a high-quality caregiver is tricky; keeping a high-quality caregiver can be more difficult since turnover in this field is high. Figure out ways to keep a high-quality caregiver motivated and attached to your child. Periodically bake her or him cookies. Invite your child to draw a picture or write a thank-you card. Present a gift certificate. Invite the person over for dinner.

Curiosity

It's raining, and there is no thunder or lightning. What will your child discover if you take a walk in the rain?

Preschoolers love new experiences, and their curiosity expands when they do something new. For a preschooler who has never taken a walk in the rain, the puddles, the worms that emerge out of the ground, and the pitter-patter of the raindrops will all get her mind going. As long as your child is safe, let your child explore.

A major barrier to curiosity is limited time. When we become rushed and scheduled, we don't have time to wonder, investigate, and experiment. Preschoolers need time to follow their interests and to see what happens if they try something new. (That's why you may unexpectedly find one of your drawers or closet shelves emptied out for no apparent reason.)

Playing with your child and giving your child age-appropriate toys will help her curiosity grow. In fact, researchers Bettye Caldwell and Robert Bradley have found that children whose parents play with them and provide high-quality toys are more likely to do well in school. High-quality toys are stimulating toys such as building blocks, dress-up clothes, large beads to string, preschool instruments, preschool puzzles, and artistic supplies, such as Play-Doh® and paints.

Time Together

Foster your child's curiosity by taking him to different places and allowing him to explore different types of toys and items. You might be surprised at what sparks a preschooler's curiosity. Try these ideas:

1. Let your child take the lead when you visit zoos, parks, playgrounds, and other interesting places. You may think a polar bear at the zoo is much more riveting than an ant hill in the middle of the sidewalk, but if your child becomes fascinated by the ant hill, follow your child's curiosity.

BONUS IDEA

Curiosity Challenge

Get a bunch of a single item (such as chenille craft stems or pieces of paper) and ask your child to create as many different things as possible. For example, a child might come up with these ideas from the chenille craft stems: a circle, a zig zag, the number one, a snake, a bracelet, or their name.

---

2. Give your child many opportunities to learn, but don't push your child. Some preschoolers enjoy learning the alphabet, others don't. Nurture your child's *curiosity* rather than trying to *control* her learning. One preschooler may spend a lot of time drawing. Another will like throwing balls and climbing. Another will recite numbers. All of these are examples of learning, and one is not better than the other. Your child will learn more by choosing to focus on what she enjoys.

3. Read aloud to your child every day. Foster your child's curiosity through interesting stories and fascinating picture books.

4. Make the ridiculous a part of your day. Preschoolers

love silliness. Make up outlandish stories, such as a fish falling up through the ceiling or monkeys visiting for lunch.

5. Give your child lots of raw materials and see what he creates. For example, a child can create a castle or a city of buildings out of cardboard boxes. A child might create a campfire out of chopsticks and red construction paper that he rips into tiny pieces. An empty egg carton might become a boat for small animals. Aluminum foil can be molded into the shape of a robot.

Discipline

The preschool years open up a new side of children that parents have often not seen before: the defiant, mean, stubborn, and aggressive side. Although toddlers are known for saying "no," preschoolers can whine, cry, hit, kick, scream, and throw a long tantrum that will embarrass, wear out, and baffle the best of parents. Most parents find themselves seeking out new techniques to discipline their preschooler while trying to figure out what happened to that delightful baby and toddler they used to know.

"Discipline means teaching, not punishment," says T. Berry Brazelton, a pediatrician and child-development expert. Although punishment may appear to work in the short term, it usually teaches children that those who have power can force others to do what they want. Ideally you want to offer guidance, structure, and understandable consequences that result in desirable behavior. When you're disciplining preschoolers in an educational way, you want to teach them positive values, social manners, and principles.

Your child is growing up. That's great and exciting when your child discovers colors, numbers, shapes, and alphabet letters. It's painful when you're on the receiving end of a child stumbling into new emotions and sensations she has never experienced—or processed—before. In essence, your child is becoming more of an individual, and you're discovering (even more so) that children cannot be controlled.

The good news about children growing up is that parents get to grow up with them. You're a professional parent of infants and toddlers. Parenting a preschooler is something new for you. So cut yourself some slack and

---

SPOTLIGHT ON ASSETS

Asset 12: Boundaries in Child-Care and Educational Settings

Discipline is much more effective when all the adults in a child's life give consistent messages. If your child is enrolled in a preschool, child-care center, or extra-curricular activity, ask for the list of rules. If possible, try to select a program with boundaries that are consistent with your rules at home; you might also choose to adjust some of your boundaries to reflect the program's rules. Making this effort results in predictable expectations and consequences, and your child will be more likely to follow the rules that are the same at home and away from home.

proceed slowly. You'll figure out the most effective way of disciplining your preschooler (and it may be different for each child or from what another parent finds effective). Listen more. React less. Try different techniques. Above all, work on creating a positive relationship with your child. It's always easier to set and enforce boundaries when there's a strong relationship.

Time Together

Instead of viewing discipline as something you do to your child (in response to something your child has done), see it as something you do together. Granted, you're hoping to convince your child to change his behavior, but discipline is part of your relationship that has a lot of give and take. Try these suggestions:

1. When disciplining your child, focus on what you want to *teach* your child rather than how you want to *punish* your child. Yelling, spanking, lecturing, taking away toys, nagging, threatening, and bribing will only create power struggles that create a clear winner and a clear loser. (And who wants to lose?) Instead, use a firm yet gentle voice that clearly teaches your child how to behave.

2. Remember how your parents disciplined you when you were a child. What was effective? What wasn't? How does your past affect your discipline methods as a parent now?

3. When tempers flare, give yourself a time out instead of your child. Say, "I'm mad, and I can't think straight. Let's talk later when I've calmed down." Leave the room. Model how you want your child to deal with intense emotion.

4. Be specific. If you don't want your child to hit,
say, "Do not hit others when you're mad. Use your words
instead." Help your child verbalize what specifically has
made her upset. Try to offer a couple of options for expressing anger or help your child find words to describe
the frustration.

5. When it comes to issues of safety, you may need to
intervene immediately and give the strong message that
your child needs to listen to you right away. For example,
if your child should suddenly sprint away from you into
a busy street, you might run after him and grab his arm
while firmly exclaiming, "No!" Once the danger has
passed, spend some time talking about the urgency of the
specific situation and the importance of safety in general.

Doctor and Dentist Visits

One key to smoother doctor and dentist visits is preparation. Even though children see doctors from birth onward, they may associate a visit to the doctor with always getting a shot because of all the immunizations. Preschoolers often don't know what to expect from a dentist, since many children don't visit a dentist before the age of three.

Even though you may not know exactly what will happen at an appointment, talk about what you do know. If your child seems anxious, explain that some people feel afraid or nervous about an appointment. Encourage your child to bring a favorite stuffed animal or toy that comforts her.

Before your child's first dentist appointment, take turns counting each other's teeth (since that's what the dentist often will do). Brush your child's teeth and talk about how a teeth cleaning can feel ticklish or a little strange because someone is bumping around on his teeth. Bring your child along during a routine appointment for an older sibling or yourself to make the experience more familiar. Explain what you love about the dentist—and why.

The more laid back you are about taking your child to the dentist and doctor, the more likely your child will be calm. But don't be surprised if your child freaks out and creates a scene. A number of preschoolers do, so don't take it personally if the visit becomes a disaster. All this is new to your child, and you can try again during your child's next visit.

Time Together

Although you cannot control how your child will act at an appointment, you can do a number of things that may make it go more smoothly. Try these ideas:

1. Ask other parents for recommendations of child-friendly doctors and dentists. When children like the health-care professionals they see, they'll be less likely to resist going.

2. Carefully choose a dental hygienist and nurse within a clinic since a child typically spends more time with these people than with doctors and dentists. If you're not allowed to choose, find out which days and hours your favorite hygienist or nurse works. Then make appointments during those times.

SPOTLIGHT ON ASSETS

Asset 7: Community Cherishes and Values Young Children

When you find a health-care provider in your community who treats children well, you're identifying another caring adult who builds assets. Doctors and dentists who give children choices in their health care (such as choosing which flavor of fluoride or which bandage design to place over a shot or blood-work prick) empower children to make their own decisions.

Bring Some Fun

Some preschoolers become upset and irritated by the glaring lights of a dental visit. Have your child bring his sunglasses and wear them in the dentist chair.

At the doctor's office, the examination table is usually covered with paper. Ask a nurse if it's okay to bring crayons and "decorate" the paper while waiting to see the doctor.

3. Be clear about how you expect your child to act. Some preschoolers become so afraid of shots or certain procedures that they can knock over items in a room while attempting to hide or escape. Acknowledge that some procedures may be uncomfortable, but emphasize that you are there to provide support. Encourage your child to squeeze your hand or hug a favorite stuffed animal.

4. Bring a new, interesting book (or a few of them) to read aloud to your child in the waiting room.

5. Play doctor or dentist with your child. Let your child wrap your imaginary broken leg with a roll of cheap toilet paper. Have your child be the dentist and show you how to brush your teeth.

Dressing

"I can do it myself!"

You'll hear your child say that over and over when it's time to get dressed, and you won't be convinced when your child emerges with missed buttons, socks of different colors, and a shirt worn inside out. What's important at this age isn't the result but the fact that your child is trying and believes she can do it.

Point out what your child is doing right, even if you want to criticize and correct. Not everything is mismatched or backward. Your child is getting some of it right, and he will feel proud when you notice.

Remember that it takes a long time and many practices for your child to master a skill. Dressing is only one of the many skills your preschooler needs to master. Go slowly. Go gently. And look for signs of progress along the way.

SPOTLIGHT ON ASSETS

Asset 20: Time at Home

What you do at home, especially during everyday routines, helps your child grow into a healthy individual. Become playful as your child gets dressed so that he enjoys the process more. If your child missed a button, say, "I see a missed button. Can you find it before I count to 20?" Close your eyes and count slowly. Most preschoolers love to surprise their parents.

Time Together

You'll be surprised how many skills are required to get dressed. There are buttons to master, zippers, snaps, bows to tie, and fabric to fit in just the right place. To assist your child in getting dressed, try these ideas:

1. If you don't like the clothes your child chooses to wear, create two complete outfits (with top, bottom, socks, and underwear) the night before. In the morning, ask your child to choose one outfit or the other. Giving your child control of this choice can save you from a stubborn battle on a busy morning.

2. Add extra time if your child is working on dressing herself. It takes a child many attempts (and lots of time) to learn how to maneuver through all the buttons, zippers, and snaps.

3. Take your child shopping for clothes. Let him choose which clothes to try on and eventually buy. Teach your child that some clothes may look good on display but don't feel comfortable to wear.

BONUS IDEA

Play Dress Up Together

Everyone knows that preschoolers love to play dress up and wear a parent's clothes. Join in on the fun. What outrageous outfit can you create? (Or which outfit haven't you worn in a long time that you'd dare to try again?) After you both dress up, make up a crazy tale about the adventure you could take in your wild outfits.

---

4. Occasionally let your child be creative with dressing. Have a backward day and encourage your child to wear her clothes backward. (This actually helps teach your child how to dress since you have to know what's backward—and what's not—to do this.) If your child insists on wearing a Batman or princess costume during the day, occasionally allow her to do this.

5. For formal occasions, have your preschooler get dressed with you. Explain what's different about dressing up for a special occasion. Take photographs.

Eating

If you're not happy with your preschooler's eating habits, you're far from alone. Preschoolers are not consistent when it comes to eating. Although their appetite tends to be stronger around ages 3 and 5 (and less strong in between), they go on food jags (when they want to eat the same food over and over) and develop food aversions (they refuse to eat certain foods). If you're not careful, mealtimes can become battlegrounds that escalate with every meal.

Experts in the field of child development suggest being patient with preschoolers and their eating habits. "Try to be, or at least appear to be, extremely relaxed about and even uninterested in the type of food eaten, *amount* of food eaten, and manner of eating," write Louise Bates Ames, Ph.D. and Frances Ilg, M.D., authors of *Your Three-Year-Old: Friend or Enemy* (New York: Dell, 1980). "Make every effort to avoid any contest of wills."

Even though mealtimes may feel chaotic, send the

message that your family eats together and that everyone sits at the table together (even if it's only for a short time). Make mealtime a connecting time when family members talk and laugh. Although a number of meals may feel like lost causes, many parents say that over the long term, this strategy works. Years from now you won't remember if your child refused to eat bananas, but everyone will remember if mealtime was a relaxed, happy time for your family to get together.

SPOTLIGHT ON ASSETS

Asset 2: Positive Family Communication

Make mealtime an enjoyable time by being intentional about fun, family conversations. Some families tell a joke with each meal. Others tell a funny story. Some parents even show the cover of a new picture book and say that they'll read it to the child after the meal is over.

Time Together

A number of research studies, including William Doherty's research in his book *The Intentional Family,* show that families who eat together on a regular basis help their children grow up well. Preschoolers also have better language skills when they eat most meals with their families. Try some of these ideas to make mealtimes more meaningful:

1. Expect conflicts to occur. As preschoolers become more independent, they will want to eat in *their* way and rebel against *your* way. Be open to their ideas. If your child wants to have a picnic dinner on your living room floor, do that sometimes. If your child wants to eat in the bathtub, say no but give another alternative so that your child doesn't feel like she never has a say.

2. Don't expect your child to eat a lot of food. Keep servings small. Preschoolers often eat small amounts and want to eat many times a day. Just make sure that what your preschooler eats is healthy most of the time. If you notice weight loss or have other nutritional concerns, ask a pediatrician for advice.

3. If your child is very hungry before a meal, it's okay to give your child a small, healthy snack. Some preschoolers get so over-hungry by mealtime that they have a hard

---

BONUS IDEA

Helping Your Child with Eating Routines

Many preschoolers spend more time talking at the table than eating. They may play with their spoon and knife, wiggle, and get caught up in a wild imaginary tale where suddenly the peas land in the potatoes. Help your child learn that talking and eating are both important for mealtimes. When your child has spent a lot of time talking and playing, say, "Now it's time to focus on eating." If your child still has trouble eating, say, "After you eat five large bites, you may talk again." Little by little, your child will gradually learn how to balance talking with eating and that mealtime is an enjoyable family time.

time concentrating and settling down. Taking the edge off of their hunger once in a while can be helpful.

4. Set clear eating boundaries, but don't set up fights. If your child refuses to eat a meal, say, "I'll save your lunch. When you're hungry, let me know." An hour later, your child may beg for cookies. Calmly say, "You may have a cookie after you have eaten your lunch." If your child protests, calmly repeat the boundary until he either eats the saved lunch or gives up on getting cookies. (If your child agrees to eat, sit next to him to show your support and to demonstrate that family members eat together.) Don't become alarmed if your child doesn't eat for a period of time. (Your child won't starve, and he will eat when the time is right.) Some preschoolers have strong wills and can go a long time without eating if they're trying to get their way.

5. When mealtimes go smoothly, talk about how much fun it was to eat together and how much you enjoyed eating with your child.

Emotional Outbursts

When it comes to expressing emotions, preschoolers tend to act in the extremes. When they love something, they're cooperative. When they hate something, they'll howl. They'll drop to the floor. They'll kick. They'll scream.

You've seen temper tantrums before, but with toddlers you could at least pick them up and carry them off. Preschoolers are too big and too strong. Their emotions can whirl them out of control, and you may not know what to do.

Asset 31: Self-Regulation

Self-regulation means teaching your child how to identify his emotions and deal with emotions effectively.
Help your preschooler handle his emotions when playing with other children and adults. Read picture books
that describe emotions and show how people express
them through laughing, smiling, crying, or talking. The
more you can guide your child in this area of development, the more likely he will develop essential emotional skills that will help him succeed.

That's okay. When preschoolers become emotional,
they often don't know what to do except spin. They become overwhelmed, and their strong emotions are new
experiences for them. They melt down.

As a parent, a gift you can give your preschooler is
to help your child become aware of her emotions and
process those emotions in positive ways. See yourself
as your child's emotional coach. Talk to your child about
his feelings. Help your child correctly identify feelings.
Help your child understand her emotions. Do not judge
your child or be overly critical about emotional outbursts,
because all preschoolers have them, and you don't want
to shame your child for being normal. Instead, teach your
child how to solve problems. Instead of kicking or hitting
people, have your child hit a pillow or run around the
yard or nearby park to release some of that energy.

To process emotions well, preschoolers need a physical release of the energy as well as the skills to talk about their feelings. When you help them with both aspects of their emotions, they'll grow up to be emotionally intelligent people—individuals who are more empathetic and persistent, have more social skills, resolve more conflicts peacefully, and are more self-motivated and self-aware. Daniel Goleman, the author of *Emotional Intelligence,* (New York: Bantam Books, 2005), believes emotional intelligence matters more than IQ. His research has found that people with modest IQs and high emotional intelligence are more successful in life than people with high IQs and modest emotional intelligence. The preschool years are crucial years for nurturing these emotionally intelligent qualities and skills in children, and this is one key area where parents have much to contribute to their children's well-being.

Time Together

Think about the big picture when dealing with your child's emotions, otherwise you easily can become discouraged. Your preschooler will have many emotional outbursts between the ages of 3 and 5, and you can help your child by trying some of these ideas:

1. At first your child will express emotion through action. Label the emotions that you see your child expressing. For example, if your child hits another child, say, "You're angry. It is important to use words instead of hitting when we're mad. Let's calm down so I can find out why you're so mad."

2. Watch your child for clues and hints that signal he is beginning to get upset. You can prevent your child's emotions from getting out of control by teaching him to see which signals he gives. For example, some children get red in the face before they explode. Others begin to rock back and forth. Some get unusually quiet. At first, you may not notice a clue right before your child explodes, but over time, you'll be able to see the subtle signals.

3. When your child is calm, occasionally talk about emotions. Ask questions such as, "What makes you sad? Why?" or "What makes you mad? Why?" or "What makes you excited? Why?" Not only will this help your child learn about her own emotions, but this will also help you learn more about your child.

BONUS IDEA

Play with Stuffed Animals and Dolls

When you play with your child, use a stuffed animal or doll to talk about emotions. For example, say, "Danny the Dog is sad today. An elephant bit him. What can we say and do to help him?" Listen to how your child responds. Your child will probably incorporate this situation into her play. Praise your child for helping Danny the Dog.

---

4. Embrace your child's feelings (no matter what they are) while setting boundaries about how to act on those feelings. Healthy children are in touch with all their emotions, and they have learned how to act on them in positive ways. Whenever you can, empathize with your child. For example, "I can see why you're mad about Joey taking your toys. I would be mad too!" Then help your child work through the problem in positive, effective ways.

5. Model how to act on feelings. When you become angry and want to explode, talk about what you're feeling and say how you need to calm down. Then calm down in a respectable way.

Fears

As children grow, they become afraid of different things at different ages. Child-development experts at the Gesell Institute of Human Development have identified specific, common fears of preschoolers.

At age 3, children tend to be afraid of the dark, animals, burglars, parents going out at night, and things that look unfamiliar, such as people who look different from them, masks, monsters, and bogeymen. By age 4, children become more afraid of loud noises, such as ones made by fire engines, ambulances, and police cars. They still may be afraid of the dark, and they're more apt to be afraid of wild animals than of animals in general. They also may have fears about a parent leaving.

By age 5, children tend to have fewer fears, but their fears tend to become more concrete. They may be afraid of getting hurt, falling, or having a dog bite them. Some 5-year-olds may still be afraid of the dark or have fears about a parent leaving.

When your child is afraid, respect your child's feeling—even if you think the fear is ridiculous. (A preschooler may be afraid of an escalator or of ladybugs.) Let your child avoid what she is afraid of for a while and ask your child for more specifics about what's scaring her. Realize that all preschoolers have fears and that all preschoolers will outgrow their fears gradually as long as their parents respect those fears and don't make a big deal of them.

Time Together

Your child's fears actually signal a healthy impulse, an impulse that you want your child to follow and develop. When people feel afraid, they become more aware and they begin to protect themselves in a more intentional way. Helping your child honor his feelings while also seeing that the world, overall, is a safe place can be a tricky part of parenting a preschooler. Try these ideas:

1. Don't force your child to face her fears at this age. Preschoolers are developing at a remarkable rate, but pushing them beyond their level of readiness is detrimental. You don't throw adults who are afraid of water into a lake. Don't do it to preschoolers either.

2. Analyze the types of fears your child has and then avoid situations that could create fear in your child. For example, if your preschooler is afraid of loud sounds, do not take him to see the fireworks on Independence Day

---

SPOTLIGHT ON ASSETS

Asset 29: Honesty

Encourage your child to be honest when it comes to his fears. Sometimes preschoolers become so afraid that they cannot articulate their fears. If this happens, try to help your child name his fears so he can begin to talk about those fears honestly.

---

or Canada Day. Avoid going to military forts where cannons are detonated or professional sporting events or concerts with ear-splitting cheering.

3. If your child fears something that must be done (such as going to the dentist or doctor), say that you know she is afraid, but you'll have to work together to go. Ask your child for ideas about what could make the visit less frightening. Maybe bringing a favorite stuffed animal or promising to take her to a park or the movies afterward would help your child.

BONUS IDEA

Using Art to Deal with Fears

If your child is afraid of monsters under the bed or of the dark, have her draw a picture of her fear. Talk about how your child is bigger than her fear. Have her look at the drawing in a full-length mirror and compare who is bigger: the drawing or your child? Then suggest that she rip up the picture into small pieces, saying: "I am bigger than my fear." A gesture like this can give preschoolers a feeling of personal power.

---

4. Reflect on your own fears. What's your view of the world? Is it a dangerous place overall or a safe place? Which fears could your child be picking up from you? Some parents are so afraid of strangers that they teach their children to avoid meeting anyone new. Instead, it's better to teach children how to reach out for help and how to discern which people are safe and which ones aren't by becoming aware of the signals that people give off. For example, you could explain that it's usually okay to talk to helpful adults in public places when other people are around, and that a safe adult will not try to lure an unfamiliar child to a private place.

5. Respect your child's tendency to withdraw from something he is afraid of. (After all, that's probably the same thing you do when you are feeling scared.) Talk about and model how you deal with your fears. Explain the difference between being afraid of something that isn't harmful and something that is. Helping your child distinguish between fear and danger will help him develop asset 35: resistance skills.

Friends

Around the age of 3, most children stop ignoring other children and begin to enjoy playing with them. Preschoolers love having friends, and they often become much more skilled at cooperating with their peers.

Preschoolers, however, are still quite young, and they'll need assistance in maneuvering through the art of relationships. They'll more likely do best by playing with one child at a time, but they'll need help resolving conflicts and figuring out what to do when they're bored. They often do not have much tact. Don't be surprised during a playdate when your child tells you loudly (in front of his friend): "Send her home! I don't want to play with her anymore." Then you'll have one angry child to work with and one hurt child to console.

Like everything else, preschoolers are learning many skills, and friendship skills will take some time and practice. Although it's embarrassing when your child says something mean to a friend, remember that your child is still learning. Respond by saying, "Let's try to find something interesting to all do together." Then talk about how to treat people well by not hurting their feelings.

Often finding an interesting activity will get a friendship back on track. Soon children will be giggling and getting their imaginations going. As friendships emerge, preschoolers may even like to hug and kiss their friends. Parents can sit back and enjoy watching camaraderie and affection take shape.

SPOTLIGHT ON ASSETS

Asset 15: Positive Peer Relationships

Friendships—positive friendships—are key for your child to grow up well. You can foster healthy peer relationships by encouraging your child to make friends and play with them. Help children take turns, solve problems, share, and care for each other in positive ways so that friendships can become easier for preschoolers.

Time Together

Encourage children to develop friendships by trying some of these ideas:

1. Arrange for a playdate at your home. Invite one child over at a time, and have your child choose the friend, not you. (Your child will more likely play with someone she chooses.) Be prepared to stay close by,

> **BONUS IDEA**
>
> *Photograph Your Child's Friends*
>
> Photograph your child with her friend. Let your child display the photo in her room. Talk about how friendships are important and how friends make our lives much more fun.

since you'll need to coach and guide the playing for this age, particularly if they don't have a lot of experience with playdates.

2. When your child invites a friend over, plan for a number of different activities in different settings. If possible, get the children outside at some point. Take them to the park for a short time or have them play in a sand box. If you enjoy crafts, do a project with them when they get bored. Give them some time to choose what they want to do, but have backups ready when conflict or boredom sets in.

3. When you take your child to public places such as a park or a zoo, introduce yourself and your child to other children who are around the same age. Play together at first and then back off while you continue to supervise your child closely. If your child rarely plays with children of other races or ethnicities, being in diverse public settings can help build cultural awareness.

4. Introduce yourself to the parents of your children's friends. Write down their names and phone numbers so that you can create playdates. Get to know the parents and find out more about their family. When you're apart, talk with your child about what you liked about his friend and family.

5. Create short playdates at first. If your child has not had much experience with playdates, first plan for about two hours. If you invite a child over for a full afternoon and they don't get along after 30 minutes, you'll have a very long day with two grumpy children.

Hate-You Outbursts

"I hate you!"

The first time your child utters that phrase, you'll be shocked. Until that moment, you would never believe it could happen to you. Yet, chances are good that your child will first say those words to you sometime during the preschool years.

Does it mean that you have failed as a parent? Hardly. In fact, it's healthy for your child to say this to you. It's

SPOTLIGHT ON ASSETS

Asset 28: Integrity

To build integrity, stand up for your child and stand up for yourself when your child says, "I hate you." You want your child to be in touch with her feelings and to express herself, but you want her to do so in tactful, caring ways. Once everyone has calmed down, reenact the situation again but with more caring words and actions.

your child's way of saying he is mad. It's your child's way of saying you can't control her. It's your child's way of saying he is different from you. It means your child is turning into a unique individual, which is all part of her normal development.

Because preschoolers aren't skilled at dealing with their emotions, they'll say things that are downright mean and hurtful. Your job is to avoid overreacting, take a big breath, and help your child make sense of what he is saying.

When your child screams that she hates you, interpret the phrase for your child. Say, "You're really mad." Help your child calm down and together find out what's making your child so angry—and why your child is so mad at you. After you've talked, tell your child that it isn't nice to say she hates someone. Say you've been hurt. As your child grows, she will gradually learn how to be more tactful and more articulate with feelings. Give your child a lot of practice with this because it will take a while, and give yourself some space since those words really hurt.

Time Together
Focusing on building a good relationship with your preschooler will help you (and your preschooler) with those hate-you outbursts. Try these ideas:

1. Recognize that all relationships have ups and downs, smooth times and times of conflict. Tell your child that everyone gets mad, and everyone makes mistakes by saying mean things. Encourage your child to apologize when he says hurtful things but not to apologize for having feelings.

Remember How Young Your Child Is

It's unnerving when your child shouts, "I hate you." Instead of overreacting, step back and remind yourself how young your child is. Most likely your child is exploding because he is overwhelmed. Notice when your child yells this kind of statement. Have you pushed your child too far? Is he hungry or exhausted? How can you care for your child so that he can feel less overwhelmed?

2. Teach your child not to express all of her opinions. (But teach this very slowly over a period of many years since you do want your child to learn to have opinions.) If a child hates how someone's hair looks, she doesn't need to say something. In fact, our world works better if everyone doesn't have to point out what they don't like about something.

3. Encourage your child to label things as dislikes rather than hates. Together make a list of your top three likes and top three dislikes. This helps your child learn more about himself and also begins to teach him about the power of language and how some words are easier to hear than others.

4. When your child uses the word *hate* in other settings, quickly tone down the language to teach your child better ways to express herself. When your child says she hates a girl, say, "You're angry that she stepped on your foot. That hurt. It also hurts when you tell someone you

hate them." Read aloud the book *Elbert's Bad Word* by
Audrey Wood (San Diego, CA: Harcourt Brace Jovanovich,
1988) when your child lashes out with harsh language.

5. Carefully look at your child's life if he begins hating
many things (or people) often. This often signals that
your child isn't happy. Maybe there's conflict at the preschool or with another family member. Ask questions
and learn more. Talk with other adults to ask for their
perspectives.

Hitting

When preschoolers get mad, they may hit someone. Hitting is a normal human impulse, and children who hit
need to learn how to control their behavior when they get
upset. Sometimes a preschooler will accuse another child
of hitting when the child wasn't being intentionally mean
and was merely playing rough. (Preschoolers need to be
taught about their own strength and what the boundaries
are for playing and expressing anger.)

If your child hits someone, immediately intervene.
Separate the children so that the hitting stops. Be clear
that hitting is unacceptable behavior. When your child
has calmed down, find out why she hit someone. Affirm
that it's okay to get angry but that it isn't okay to hit. If
you discover the child wasn't intentionally trying to hurt
the other child and was merely playing rough, be clear
that playing needs to be gentle and not hurt other people.

Although occasional hitting is normal for preschoolers, frequent attacks are not. Seek professional help by
visiting your pediatrician, a psychologist, or another child-

care expert if your child lashes out without being provoked, never feels sorry, blames others for his hitting, or is easily angered. Letting this behavior slide will only lead to more serious problems that will be difficult to alter when your child is older.

Time Together

Although it's horrifying to watch your child hit someone, be careful not to shame your child. It's important to intervene and to teach your child better ways to behave, but it's never okay to belittle your child, even if she misbehaves. Try these ideas:

1. Sometimes children go through a brief period of hitting, especially if they're tired or stressed. If your child isn't making progress from your interventions and teachings after about a month, seek guidance from your pediatrician.

2. Immediately intervene every time your child hits so that he understands what he is doing wrong and how to act instead.

3. Teach your child to use words instead of fists. Encourage your child to walk away and take a break when angry feelings pulse through her body. Praise your child every time you see her making positive choices.

4. Monitor your child so that he doesn't substitute another aggressive behavior for hitting. Be clear that biting, kicking, and pushing are just as unacceptable as hitting. Once they've calmed down, encourage children to use positive physical gestures, such as hugging or shaking hands, to express forgiveness.

5. Always give a positive, simple alternative that your child can use instead of hitting. For example, say, "Instead of hitting, take a deep breath and say that you're mad."

BONUS IDEA

Establish Clear Rules

Closely analyze which behaviors your preschooler needs to unlearn. Set three rules and repeat them often. One parent set these rules: No hitting, no sticking out tongues, and no name calling. Another parent, whose preschooler liked to hit, set these three rules: no hitting, no hitting, and no hitting.

Holidays and Family Gatherings

Because of their great imagination and enthusiasm, pre-schoolers can be delightful companions during holidays and family gatherings. Unfortunately, with all the hype and anticipation, adults can inadvertently overexcite a preschooler, which can lead to a disastrous day.

Preschoolers are quick to note which gatherings and holidays are most important to a family. They're the ones that require much preparation, sometimes days (or weeks) in advance. Annual holiday events appear, and a lot of activity can center around food preparation, decorating, and even gift giving. These can range from Thanksgiving to family reunions to family birthday gatherings.

Although family gatherings and holidays are special events, it's wise to try to maintain your daily routines with your preschooler. All the new activity (which won't seem new to you because it happens every year) can overwhelm a preschooler. If you add these new activities while also preserving wake-up times, mealtimes, nap times, bath times, playtimes, and bedtimes, you'll help your child be less stressed for family gatherings and holidays.

Time Together

Holidays can be a wonderful time for a family to connect—as long as the stress levels are kept low for everyone involved. Try these ideas to make your next holiday a smooth occasion:

1. Since preschoolers don't have the ability to tell time and day like adults do, make countdowns to a holiday concrete. Some families create a visual wall calendar where a child adds a sticker or crosses out each day that leads to a holiday. Others create a paper chain where the child can remove one link of the chain before bed each night and count the number of chains in the morning to see how many days are left until the holiday arrives.

2. Be intentional about which holiday traditions you keep and which ones can wait a few years until your children are older. Holidays can easily overwhelm the most organized adult. Keep your stress levels low so that your child will stay relaxed and enjoy the celebration. Choose holiday traditions that will be most meaningful to you and your child.

SPOTLIGHT ON ASSETS

Asset 3: Other Adult Relationships

Family gatherings and holidays are an ideal time to encourage other adults to connect with your preschooler. If other adults don't initiate an activity during the holidays, create opportunities yourself. For example, one family always visited a great-grandmother during the holidays each year and brought along preschool games to play together. Another family invited the neighbors over for a holiday snack to celebrate and get to know them better.

---

3. A number of holidays have ties to faith communities. Choose a religious service that fits your family well and talk with your child about why you attend a religious service during the holidays. It is valuable for preschoolers to feel connected to a religious community.

4. People often think of others who are less fortunate

during holidays. Try to create one project where you and your child can help someone in a caring, meaningful way. Some families bake cookies to give away. Others sing songs at an assisted-living center. Others visit extended family members who are homebound due to illness. If you encourage your child to donate old toys to a charitable thrift store, you can also enjoy knowing there will be more room for storing new gifts.

5. Remember to stop and play with your child. During the holidays, it's easy to get caught up in the long to-do lists and to think that playing is frivolous. Preschoolers thrive when their parents play with them, and they'll enjoy the holidays more if you take the time to hang out with them in ways that preschoolers love best.

Imaginary Play

Preschoolers make up the wildest tales, and they can get caught up in the drama and dress up of their imaginations. Their creative imaginations delight most adults— until the imagination seems to go too far.

What do you do if your child spends more time in her imagination than in reality? What if your child's imaginary play includes violent themes? What if your child's best friend is an imaginary friend? What if your child enjoys the company of imaginary friends more than real people?

Questions such as these often perplex parents of preschoolers. The good news, however, is that imaginary play is critical to your child's healthy development. Children cannot distinguish between fantasy and real life

---

SPOTLIGHT ON ASSETS

Asset 22: Engagement in Learning Experiences

Provide your child with a variety of toys and supplies that stimulate her imagination, which can make her feel more engaged in learning experiences. For example, give your child a costume box, doctor kit, construction toys (such as LEGO® blocks, Lincoln Logs®, or Tinkertoy® sets), and housekeeping toys. Think beyond the usual art supplies; egg cartons, cereal boxes, coffee filters, empty yogurt containers, and paper towel tubes are great for making creative crafts. Make learning a fun time for your child.

during the preschool years, so expect your child's imagination to make up a lot of his day. If your child starts including a lot of violent themes, ask about it. Sometimes children process their fears, their sense of power (or lack of power), and their new feelings through their imagination. As long as they aren't hurting themselves or others—or becoming overly obsessed with a certain theme—most of the time, it's okay. It's developmentally on track.

Time Together

Stepping into your child's imaginary world from time to time will help you connect more with your preschooler. Try some of these ideas:

1. When your child asks you to play with her, join in even if it feels a bit ridiculous. Your child may say, "You're the cow. Say moo." Play along with your child's imagination. If your child rarely invites you to play, ask if you can play. (Children love to play with adults.)

2. If your preschooler has an imaginary friend, occasionally encourage your child to be kind and helpful to this friend. You may be surprised to see a side of your child you've never seen before.

3. Your child's imaginary play helps his brain to develop, so encourage the imaginary play to continue when you're running errands together. Ask your child to bring his favorite stuffed animal. Sometimes your child's imagination will take off even more when accompanied by a furry friend.

4. When your child plays with another friend, occasionally eavesdrop on their imaginary play. It's delightful how quickly children can go from being robbers to being rabbits to landing on the moon to changing a baby's diaper. If two children play well together, tell them how happy you are about that.

5. If your child's imaginary friend becomes stubborn and uncooperative (which leads to your child becoming uncooperative), become creative in ways to invite the imaginary friend to do things that your child usually objects to. For example, say, "I love how Leon (the imaginary friend) helps me find snacks at the grocery store. You and Leon might like to come with me to the grocery store."

Intensity

Preschoolers have abundant energy. They're going all the time. They're intense, but sometimes they may seem too energetic and too intense.

With all the news about attention-deficit/hyperactivity disorder (ADHD), sometimes it's easy to be convinced that your preschooler has a problem. Yet, that may not be true. Your child may be acting like a preschooler should. Or your child may have a personality that's more intense and a body that needs to go, go, go.

Typical preschool development means that your child may be bouncing off the walls at times and get so excited that she has a hard time concentrating on one thing for very long. Those with ADHD are even more active, have even shorter attention spans, and also display other symptoms.

If you're ever unsure about your child's intensity, ask your pediatrician. Most of the time, what you're observing will be normal behavior for this age group. If your pediatrician detects something more, he or she will refer you to the help your child needs.

Time Together

Begin to see intensity as a gift instead of a curse (even if your child wears you out). An intense child typically is enthusiastic about learning and being active in all kinds of pastimes. To help you deal with your child's intensity, try a few of these ideas:

1. Work with your child's intensity instead of pushing against it. Instead of becoming frustrated that your child won't eat triangle-shaped toast, make another piece and cut it in the way your child prefers. (Remember: Besides being intense, preschoolers are also asserting themselves and discovering their personal preferences.)

2. Just because your child is intense doesn't mean that *you* need to be intense. Take frequent breaks. Focus on keeping yourself calm. Your energy and stress levels affect your child. A calm parent often helps take the edge off an intense preschooler.

3. Observe other preschoolers. How intense and energetic are they? How is each one intense in his own way? How is your child unique? A lot of preschool intensity is

---

BONUS IDEA

Learn More about Intensity

Two helpful books can provide more information (and practical tips) on parenting an intense child. *Raising Your Spirited Child: A Guide for Parents Whose Child Is More Intensive, Sensitive, Perceptive, Persistent, Energetic* by Mary Sheedy Kurcinka (New York: HarperCollins, 1991) helps you see the gift of your child's intensity. Another book, *Living with the Active Alert Child* by Linda S. Budd, Ph.D. (Seattle: Parenting Press, 1993, 2003) gives strategies for children who are frequently misdiagnosed as hyperactive or learning disabled.

---

normal, and you'll see a variety of ways that preschoolers express their intensity.

4. Give your child a quiet time every day. Set a kitchen timer together and help her select books or quiet toys to enjoy in a calm area of the house. Even though your child is intense, your child needs to learn how to slow down and do soothing, quiet activities. Be patient if this is difficult for your child. Think of being calm as a skill that you're gradually teaching your child.

5. Expect a lot of intense expressions of emotion. Your preschooler often gets overwhelmed with his feelings, and he has not learned the skills yet for dealing with all these different sensations and moods. Be patient. Help your child articulate his feelings. Teach your child positive ways to behave and express emotions.

Intergenerational Relationships

It's easy to create an age-segregated world with preschoolers. Many attend a child-care center or preschool, and those who don't tend to have playdates with other preschoolers.

Research clearly shows the benefits of intergenerational relationships. Preschoolers who have connections with people from many generations expand their network of supportive adults beyond their parents and caregivers, and people from other generations often bring out wonderful sides of preschoolers. For example, one preschooler insisted on taking a walk every day near a neighbor's house because the elderly man always greeted the boy and let him play with his dog. Another preschooler liked visiting her aunt in college because the two ordered pizza together and ate it on the floor on top of a blanket. A preschooler with a teenage brother may be excited to learn the names of his brother's best friends and might clap when they arrive to tousle his hair and carry him around.

Over the long term, individuals from different generations can serve as strong advocates for you and your family. They can help you weather hard times and give you perspective when you or your child feel overwhelmed. In the short term, they provide support and friendship, which benefits not only your child but also your entire family.

SPOTLIGHT ON ASSETS

Asset 14: Adult Role Models

When your child gets to know people of other generations, those adults become role models. Although preschoolers tend to see the adults in their families as their top role models, they also need other adults to look up to. Encourage your child to get to know respectable teachers, child-care providers, and neighbors who can influence your child in positive ways.

Time Together

Children grow up better when they're involved in a supportive network of adults. Intergenerational relationships can widen their network. Try some of these ideas:

1. If an extended family member takes an interest in your preschooler, periodically invite that person over to build the relationship more. Grandparents, aunts, uncles, and even older cousins can have a big impact on a preschool-age child. If you have older children, invite them to plan "special" time with the preschooler in your family.

2. Attend block parties and other neighborhood gatherings to get to know your neighbors. Introduce your preschooler to people of all ages in your neighborhood.

3. Invite people of other generations over for a meal. Some families do this once a month as a way for their family to get to know other people better.

4. Become involved in a religious community. Search Institute President Peter Benson says, "Religious institutions are one of the few remaining intergenerational communities to which youth have access." Faith communities can be great places to meet friends of all ages.

5. Buy an extra season ticket to children's theater, zoo, children's museum, or children's orchestra concert series. Invite someone of another generation to join you and your preschooler.

Jealousy

Family life can be somewhat smooth—until you add someone new. Whether another child—or another adult—joins your family, you'll soon find yourself dealing with your child's jealousy.

Whenever roles change, children (and adults) feel unsure of themselves. They want life to stay the same because it was comfortable and clear. They knew where they stood, and they knew how to get your attention.

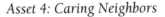

SPOTLIGHT ON ASSETS

Asset 4: Caring Neighbors

Sometimes finding another caring adult to pay attention to your child can help your child's jealousy—especially when a new sibling arrives and seems to attract all the interest of adults. Recruit the help of a caring neighbor who is willing to reach out to your preschooler. Even if a neighbor doesn't spend a lot of time with your child, a little bit of attention can go a long way. Preschoolers feel special when adults around them notice them.

The addition of a baby can bring out a lot of jealousy in an older sibling since the infant requires a lot of care. An older, more independent preschooler may feel left out and begin to pick on and act mean toward the baby.

BONUS IDEA

Draw the Jealousy Monster

Everyone feels jealous. Even adults. Tell that to your preschooler. Explain that feeling jealous is normal. Then teach your preschooler that jealousy can become like a big monster if he doesn't talk about jealous feelings. Together, draw pictures of the jealousy monster. Describe your pictures and talk about your monsters with each other.

Preschoolers may also become jealous when a single parent starts dating—and when a single parent gets married. Preschoolers know where all the attention is going (especially when they're not on the receiving end). It's best to acknowledge your preschooler's feelings and to create times when the three of you are together and your preschooler is the center of attention.

Keep giving your preschooler individual attention and talk about your family when you are all going through a transition. Take out your preschooler's baby photos (or adoption arrival photos) and show them to him. Talk about how happy you were when he joined your family. Explain how much you love him—just as much now as you did then. Over time, jealousy most likely will subside.

Time Together

Every child will feel jealous from time to time and will act out that jealousy. Here are some ideas on how to deal with jealousy in positive ways:

1. Children become less jealous when their needs are met. On a regular basis throughout the day, give your child your undivided attention.

2. Feelings of jealousy are exacerbated by the fact that preschoolers are self-centered. Most think the world revolves around them, and they become upset when it doesn't. Teach your child that she is important, but other family members are just as important.

3. Never let your preschooler spend time alone with a younger sibling or baby. Even if your preschooler is good natured, preschoolers can become aggressive and hurt a younger sibling. Preschoolers need constant supervision.

4. Hire a baby-sitter on a more regular basis when an infant joins your family. Sometimes have the sitter stay with your infant while you do something alone with your preschooler. Or find a sitter whom your preschooler especially adores to give him a lot of attention.

5. Don't be surprised if your preschooler begins to act like a baby or toddler if you add an infant to your family. Preschoolers quickly see how much they enjoyed—and now miss—some of the aspects of being younger. Allow your child some space to work through her feelings. Talk about the positive aspects of being young and also of growing up.

Kindergarten, Getting Ready for

Is your child ready for kindergarten? That's the question on most parents' minds when they have preschoolers, and many parents spend a lot of time during the preschool years helping their children prepare for elementary school.

Unfortunately, most parents emphasize certain skills more than others, and children need to have a wide variety of skills to begin kindergarten successfully. States, provinces, and school districts have varying criteria, so contact your local school district to find out about requirements. Even if your child is only 3, contacting them now will help you prepare well.

Most parents try to teach their children the alphabet and how to count. Although this is helpful, most educators believe that parents are overemphasizing memorization and placing too little emphasis on other skills. Educators also look for how a child uses a pencil, traces basic shapes, and uses a pair of scissors (fine motor skills). They want children who can separate from a parent, follow rules, and play with another child (social skills). They look for children who can skip, bounce a ball, and walk backward (gross motor skills). They hope that children can identify some alphabet letters and can recognize certain colors and shapes (academic skills). They also want children to be able to tell how old they are, know their entire name, and identify their address and telephone number (personal information).

Since each child develops differently, some children will have skills that are stronger in certain areas (such as gross motor) and weaker in others (fine motor). As a parent, it's best to give your child a wide variety of experiences to help him learn rather than pushing him to memorize specific information. What you want is a happy, curious child who is eager to go to kindergarten when the time is right.

Time Together

Helping your child get ready for kindergarten is not a competition. It's about helping your child develop in a well-rounded way so that she can't wait to go to school. Try some of these ideas:

1. Make books a part of your daily life. Read aloud to your child. Take him to the library on a regular basis. Go to community story times. Have your child listen to books on audiocassette or compact disc. Create plays out of stories you read. The more you immerse your child in reading, the better off he will be academically.

2. Contact your school district to see if your child is required to take a preschool screening test. Some school districts will even allow your child to take the test a number of times at different ages. These tests can help you learn which skills your child has mastered and which ones you can help her develop. In addition, find out when your child needs a thorough physical examination to attend kindergarten. (Most states and provinces require this.) Your pediatrician also can help you identify how your child is developing.

3. Take an active role in your child's learning and growth. Whether your child goes to a preschool or stays at home with you, your involvement and enthusiasm will make a big difference.

4. Let your child play, play, play. Preschoolers learn mainly through play, so give your child as many opportunities to play as you can.

5. Relax. Preschoolers change so quickly that they can begin to do things one week that they couldn't the week before. Just continue to give your child a lot of opportunities to play, practice, and explore.

Lying

Preschoolers lie. Preschoolers exaggerate. If you're having trouble because your preschooler is not being truthful, you are far from alone.

Preschoolers lie for many reasons. Most do so because their imagination is large, and they have a hard time distinguishing between fact and fantasy. Thus, you can get a wild story about how the cookies in the cookie jar all disappeared without your preschooler touching them.

At the same time, preschoolers are also old enough to learn why people lie. They want to avoid getting into trouble. A 1998 study of 3- to 5-year-olds at Pitzer College in Claremont, California, revealed that children as young as 3 have enough social savvy to know that sometimes it's better to hide your true feelings and not tell the truth, which is the basis for telling white lies.

Responding to a lying preschooler can be tricky. First determine whether your child is caught in a fantastical tale. If so, don't fuss too much. (You can, however, be clear that lying isn't acceptable.) If your child is learning to lie from an adult, however, then the lying needs to stop— by both the adult and the child.

Continue to teach the difference between right and wrong, but don't expect your child to learn quickly. Honesty is a positive value, and it takes children many years to learn and begin to act in ways that adults value. Be patient, and never call your child a liar. Continue teaching, and gradually your child should begin to tell the truth on a more regular basis.

SPOTLIGHT ON ASSETS

Asset 29: Honesty

The way you respond to your child's dishonesty will teach your child a lot about lying and honesty. Don't blow up. Don't hand out harsh punishment. If you want to teach your child to be more honest, emphasize the importance of telling the truth more than the offense at hand. When you do that, your child will learn the positive value of honesty.

Time Together

Since lying is so common among preschoolers, try these ideas to teach your child how to tell the truth:

1. Whenever you witness someone telling the truth, point out how you think that's a good thing. Explain how hard it is to be honest sometimes, and that it's admirable to tell the truth.

2. Be honest, but remain calm. If your child colored on the walls and blamed her sister, acknowledge the complexity of the situation. Say something like: "I can see why you blamed your sister. You didn't want to get into trouble. You knew I would get upset with coloring on the wall, and you're right. We don't color on walls. But, it's just as important to tell the truth. In the future, I want you to be honest. Now, how can we figure out what to do about these walls?" Teaching positive values requires supporting your child and giving clear boundaries while also emphasizing the power of honesty.

3. Lying is common among adults, and you probably bend the truth in certain areas. Do you know where? Watch for nuances in your language. We may think we're trying to protect our child when we say, "That won't hurt,"

BONUS IDEA

Tell the Truth (Gently) about Your Child's Lies

As an adult, it's often easy to tell when your preschooler lies. If your child says he made it to the bathroom in time, but his pants are soaked, it's rather obvious what happened. Instead of disagreeing with your child and pointing out the lie, say something about the truth. For example, calmly say, "It looks like you didn't make it to the bathroom in time. That can happen to anyone. Let's get you changed into dry clothes. Next time, it would be helpful if you told me about it."

---

yet we're stretching the truth. How often do you say, "Just a minute," when, in reality, you need your child to wait much longer? Watch what you do so that you can set a good example and be a positive role model.

4. Teach children to be honest with themselves. Honesty isn't just about what you do with other people, it's also how you act when you're alone. Some children learn that it's okay to lie if they don't get caught. Instead, teach them that how they act all the time—whether they're alone or with people and whether or not they get caught— is what matters most.

5. Help your child become more aware of what's fantasy and what's reality. Although this concept will be over most preschoolers' heads, they can begin to learn the difference gradually. For example, when your child tells a friend that your family is moving into a mansion (when you're not moving at all), say something like, "It's fun to imagine living in a mansion isn't it? Make sure you tell your friend when you're using your imagination and when you're talking about something that's real."

Media Use

Television. Movies. Videos. Computers. Internet. Video games. We're surrounded by media, and so are our children. As a parent, you can control your child's media use, and it's wise to do so. "If we orient our kids to screens so early in their lives, we risk making media their automatic default activity," says Dr. David Walsh, president and founder of the National Institute on Media and the Family.

Many parents use the media to help with parenting. It's easy to stick a preschooler in front of the TV or the computer, and you know your child will stay there and not wander off. As long as you do this once in a while (and as long as you're controlling what your child is watching and doing), that's okay.

Do not, however, use media as a second parent. Even though it may seem to make your parenting role easier in the short term, it will make it much more difficult in the long term. "We urge parents to limit the amount of TV that their children view, to monitor what their children are watching, and to watch TV with them to help them learn from what they see," says the American Academy of Pediatrics in its book, *Caring for Your Baby and Young Child: Birth to Age 5* (New York: Bantam Books, 2004). "We believe that televised violence has a clear effect upon the behavior of children and contributes to the frequency with which violence is used to resolve conflict."

Choose your child's media influences carefully. Through television shows on public broadcasting stations around the world, preschoolers learn basic skills. (In the United States, the major broadcaster is PBS. In Canada, it's the national CBC.) Educational preschool computer games also are valuable. The Center on Media and Child Health, however, found that "studies indicate that even the youngest children in the United States are using a wide variety of screen media, many at higher levels than recommended by child-development professionals." By keeping tabs on *what* your preschooler is watching as well as *how much time* your preschooler is spending in front of a screen, you can make media use a positive factor in your child's life.

Time Together

Media use works well when you control and monitor its use. Try these ideas to get the most benefits from media use:

1. Set clear guidelines about how much media your child can use in a day. For example, let your child watch a 30-minute educational children's show on TV and then turn off the TV and do a different activity. If your child plays computer or video games, set a timer. Give your child a five-minute warning before the computer or video game needs to be turned off. Some parents do not let their preschoolers turn on any media (such as TV or computer) without a parent's permission.

2. If your child attends a child-care center or a pre-school, find out how much electronic media is used.

(Some caregivers have a TV on at all times.) Make sure there are clear boundaries around media use, and that the climate is nurturing and stimulating.

3. Do not allow your child to have any type of electronic media (other than a radio or CD player) in his room. Research clearly shows that children who have a TV in their rooms watch more TV than their peers, and they read (or are read to) less.

BONUS IDEA

Have a Day without the Media

Occasionally take a day when you turn off all the media in your home. (Make sure you do this on a day where you have more flexibility and time to spend with your child.) Play games together. Create imaginary tales. Read books together. Visit the zoo, the library, or a children's museum. You have countless opportunities for fun—without the media.

---

4. Never let your child watch a PG-13, R, NC-17, or X-rated movie, or a TV-7 or TV-14 show, even if it's with you and you know your child doesn't understand the adult content. (Make sure baby-sitters and child-care providers don't do this either.) Your child is too young to make sense of people dying, getting sick, or getting pregnant; they simply see confusing messages about drug, alcohol, and tobacco use; sexuality; and violence. They will learn that risky behaviors are positive ways to act.

5. Monitor the balance between your child's media use and book use. TV and computer use should be limited compared to the time your child spends reading and playing. Also give your child opportunities to play with other children. Your child will learn more by playing with other children and reading books than by sitting in front of the TV or computer screen.

Moving

You're planning to move. When do you tell your child? How do prepare your child for the move, especially if she has never moved before? How can you make the move go well?

Preschoolers always enjoy an adventure, so emphasizing the adventuresome side of moving will pique preschoolers' curiosity. (Be honest, though, since moving

---

SPOTLIGHT ON ASSETS

Asset 38: Self-esteem

Since your child will experience a lot of changes before, during, and after a move, work hard to keep some consistency in your lives. If you need to hire a baby-sitter while you pack, hire someone your child knows or ask an extended family member to help out. This will help your child feel valued and secure despite the busy atmosphere. Making other changes, such as hiring an unfamiliar baby-sitter, will be much more stressful and less effective when your child is also coping with the stress of a move.

also has its frustrating and sad moments, as well.) Tell your preschooler as soon as you know you're going to move, and involve your child in as much of the process as you can.

Be up front with your child about why you're moving. If you're going through a divorce, be honest about it so that your child knows what to expect. If you're getting a new job, talk about that. Or if you've been hit hard financially and need to move into a less-expensive place, tell your child that you found a place where you won't have to worry so much about money. Children always do better if they know *why* they're moving.

Whatever the reason for your move, reassure your child that he *is* and *will be* okay. Remind your preschooler that you'll still be together, and many things will remain the same. Tell your child that you're excited about your new home, and (if possible) show your child where you will be living. Highlight other benefits to your child: where the library, parks, swimming pool, and playgrounds are located near your new home.

Time Together
Moving entails a lot of work, and it's never easy for anyone. Help make the move go more smoothly for you and your child by trying a few of these ideas:

1. Create a moving bag for your child. This will include your child's most important treasures (such as a favorite stuffed animal, toy, book, and music). Preschoolers feel less out of control if they know where to find their favorite things, and they can hug a stuffed animal or doll when they feel overwhelmed during the move.

2. Display a monthly calendar with the moving date

completely colored. Each evening, have your child mark off the day and count how many days until the move. This will help your child anticipate when the move will happen.

3. If you've hired a moving company, ask if it has any resources for children. Some have coloring or activity books for young children that address the issues of moving to a new location.

4. Whenever you're making a major change, it often helps to read aloud stories on the subject. Many picture books about moving help preschoolers identify their feelings and understand what happens during a move. Ask your local librarian for book recommendations.

5. If you're moving far away and you're leaving behind friends and family, have a gathering so that you and your child get a chance to say good-bye before you go. Take photographs. Collect the addresses, phone numbers, and e-mail addresses of your friends and family, and talk with your child about how you can stay in touch—even if you're far away. Invite the important adults in your preschooler's life to try some of the ideas in *Stay Close: 40 Clever Ways to Connect with Kids When You're Apart* by Tenessa Gemelke (Minneapolis, MN: Search Institute, 2005).

Naps

Sometime between the ages of 3 and 5, most children will no longer need a nap. Since children have a lot of energy at this age, however, it's a smart idea to continue having a "quiet time" during the day so that preschoolers can unwind and even take a short nap if they need it.

The amount of sleep that preschoolers need can vary greatly from child to child, which is why one 3-year-old no longer needs a nap while another 5-year-old does. All this is normal, so do not be concerned if you notice either extreme in your child.

What may be more important for your child, however, is to have the quiet time to unwind. Preschoolers tend not to be aware of their bodies, so they can push their bodies way beyond their limits. (That's why your preschooler can be up jumping around late at night due to all the excitement of a holiday and then be sound asleep a minute later.) A quiet time helps your child slow down, relax, and do quiet things like looking at picture books or playing quietly.

Asset 16: Positive Expectations

Having a daily nap or quiet time can help your pre-schooler slow down and become more aware of her body and emotions. When you insist on a nap or quiet time, you're showing your preschooler that life is not lived at full throttle at all times. Resting gives your child a chance to calm down and recharge; this results in a more positive attitude and better behavior. Point out to your preschooler that all people perform better when they take regular breaks and slow down.

When you're with your child all day, this quiet time (or nap time) also gives you a much needed break. It's important to have some time apart, and a quiet time can provide that. Have your child go to his room for this quiet time. Turn off the lights, the music, and the stimulation and let your child nap or do quiet activities. (Preschoolers often enjoy having a book light or a flashlight if they're awake for this quiet time.) Afterward, both you and your preschooler will be refreshed and ready to tackle the rest of the day.

Time Together

A nap time (or quiet time) can become a favorite part of the day, as long as it does not become a battle time. Try these ideas to make nap and quiet times smoother and more enjoyable:

1. Make nap and quiet times a part of your everyday routine. If you don't, your child will be more apt to resist, and you'll lose the activity. Preschoolers do much better with structured days, and if they know that a nap or quiet time happens every afternoon after reading a book with you, they'll be more likely to cooperate.

2. Expect resistance to nap and quiet times. Preschoolers like to go, go, go, and they do not like to slow down. Be clear that a nap or quiet time is nonnegotiable. Give your child some interesting, quiet activities to do during this time. Parents often smile when, after much initial protesting, they find their child napping—or begging to extend a quiet time to keep playing.

3. If your child runs out of the room and refuses to have a quiet time, calmly take her by the hand and lead her back. Sometimes lying next to your child will slow her down, and you may find yourself getting a nap too!

4. At first, some children who have outgrown naps may not know how to have a quiet time. You may need to spend the first quiet time with your child to show him

---

BONUS IDEA

Teach Your Child to Slow Down

If your child struggles with quiet time and tends to be highly active, use the quiet time to teach your child to slow down. Together with your child, talk through the basics of relaxation. Lie down. Close your eyes. Slow your breathing. Feel your body relax (and not wiggle).

how to play quietly. Once a non-napping preschooler sees the possibilities of a quiet time, he'll be more likely to look forward to it and enjoy it.

5. Some children enjoy listening to quiet music during a nap or quiet time. Visit your local library and ask the librarian for audiotapes and compact discs that are helpful for naps. Your librarian will have recommendations that fit preschoolers, as well as ones that are ideal for toddlers and infants.

Nightmares and Night Terrors

Nightmares and night terrors are common for preschoolers, and these nighttime scares can disrupt your child's sleep—and yours. Young preschoolers often have a lot of difficulty with nightmares because they believe their nightmares are real. They're terrified of the monster they dreamed of because they're convinced that monster is alive and after them.

Night terrors also appear during the preschool years. Night terrors differ from nightmares because your child appears to be awake while being in a state of great distress. In fact, your child is neither awake nor having a nightmare. It's a partial arousal from a sleeping state.

Night terrors tend to happen early in the evening (about one to four hours after falling asleep), while nightmares tend to happen much later in the sleep cycle when your child is in a deep sleep. During a night terror, your child will not be aware of your presence whereas your child *will* be aware and assured by your presence after a nightmare.

Asset 1: Family Support

Give your child a lot of support if he is having frequent nightmares and night terrors. Even when they seem harmless to you, take these incidents seriously since they scare your child. Talk about your child's fears and concerns and figure out ways to help him feel more secure. For example, your child may feel better sleeping with stuffed animals that can guard him through the night. Other children would prefer to sleep with a night light. Any of these comforting items along with your reassuring words will help your child feel more supported and safe.

Whether your child has a nightmare or a night terror, it is important to offer reassurance and calm him down. With nightmares, your child may cling to you and have trouble falling back asleep, fearful of having another nightmare. Calmly reassure your child and rub his back until he falls asleep.

With a night terror, your child will probably push you away if you touch her, but you can coax your child to calm down by giving simple instructions, such as: "I am here. You are okay. You can go back to sleep." When your child calms down, she will quickly fall back asleep as if nothing had happened.

Time Together

Although night terrors will disappear as your preschooler gets older, and your child will become less afraid of nightmares, you can do a number of things to help cope with these sleeping problems:

1. Monitor your child's stress levels. Stress often can trigger bad dreams. Don't let your child watch TV before going to bed, and create a calm, soothing bedtime routine to help your child sleep better. Limiting fluids before bed may also decrease the chances that your child will awaken.

BONUS IDEA

Give Your Child a Flashlight

Some children become so afraid of nightmares that they don't want to go to sleep. If your child is afraid of storms or other noises, the sound of a fan or radio may distract her from the fear. You can also give your preschooler a sense of control by letting her sleep with a flashlight. Tell your child that she can turn on the light if a nightmare comes and wakes her up. Although your child may never actually do this, she often will feel more secure sleeping with a source of light.

---

2. Talking about nightmares with your child will often help; discussing night terrors won't. Children who have night terrors have no memory of them (or their wild behavior) in the morning.

3. If your child has a nightmare, encourage him to tell you about it. Listen closely. Ask questions. Tell your child that nightmares feel real but they are not real. Explain how nightmares stop as soon as you wake up. It's often helpful to tell your child that everybody—including adults—has nightmares.

4. Remain calm when your child is in the middle of a night terror or nightmare. Night terrors can be alarming to parents since your child often thrashes, screams, and moves in bizarre ways while having her eyes open. Although your child will resist your attempts to calm her down, remain calm and continue talking softly to her to help her.

5. As with any condition, if your child's nightmares or night terrors seem to be getting out of hand, seek the advice of your pediatrician.

Playing

What preschoolers enjoy and need to do most is play. As young preschoolers, they often need assistance from an adult and may feel frustrated when they haven't developed the skills to play as they wish. By the time they are 5 years old, they are more self-sufficient and may play more contently.

Preschoolers play to experience the world and themselves. They play to learn new things and to master certain skills. They play to discover what it's like to interact with individuals and groups of children.

To give your preschooler the best benefits of playtime, create a daily routine that's predictable and includes a lot of time for play. Vary the play so your child has some indoor time and outdoor time, time to build with blocks, art time (finger painting, coloring, cutting, or working with clay), imaginary play, music (to sing and dance), social playtime, time to run and move, and story times. The possibilities within each type of play are endless. What's essential is that the play is age appropriate and stimulating.

SPOTLIGHT ON ASSETS

Asset 18: Out-of-Home and Community Programs

Although your child spends a lot of time at home playing, you can also be on the lookout for preschool play programs. (You can often find them through community education.) These play programs expose preschoolers to new types of stimulating play and give them opportunities to play with other children the same age.

Time Together

Your preschooler will turn your home into a play area. You'll have toys strewn all around your house, and your child will be creating adventures in your bathroom, kitchen, attic, and every corner of your home. Help your child get the most out of playtime by trying some of these ideas:

1. Get basic toys for your preschooler: art supplies, balls, blocks, books, cars, modeling clay or homemade dough, dolls and stuffed animals, puzzles, and toys to use outside (such as a sandbox, wagon, and tricycle).

Collect toys that especially interest your child. (Some are fascinated with dollhouses, board games, or action figures.) You don't have to buy everything new. Second-hand stores and garage sales offer a wide range of toys at reasonable prices. Storing some toys and rotating what's available can also add to the appeal.

2. Give your preschooler opportunities to play at playgrounds and gyms. Many communities, parks, and shopping malls have indoor playground areas for preschoolers in addition to outdoor playgrounds.

3. Provide plenty of art materials for your child. Preschoolers can go through a lot of paper, so buy it in bulk or recycle photocopies with one blank side. Also consider purchasing paper in different sizes and textures since that will open up your child's imagination. Local businesses may be willing to donate recycled paper.

BONUS IDEA

Use Appliance Boxes for Playtimes

Preschoolers love climbing in boxes, and appliance boxes (for refrigerators, stoves, washing machines, and dryers) crack open preschoolers' imaginations even more. Soon they'll want additional boxes in other sizes so that they can create a town of homes and cars.

---

4. Play with your child. If you especially enjoy outdoor activities, go out and move with your child. Dance together. If you enjoy art activities, create your own art-supply stash and pull it out when your child wants to create. Some parents even purchase more complex coloring books (created for older children, teenagers, and adults) that they find stimulating for themselves.

5. Purchase costumes and oversized clothing after Halloween (when costumes are on sale) and from secondhand clothing stores. Go through your closets and jewelry boxes and pull out items you haven't worn in years. Ask extended family members if they have anything to donate. Preschoolers love to dress up.

Puzzling Behaviors

Just when you've figured out how to parent your child, your child changes. That's how a lot of parenting goes. As your child grows, you discover new things that bewilder you.

Sometimes your preschooler may develop an unusual behavior. Maybe your child starts blinking rapidly, chewing her clothes, rocking, spitting, biting his nails, drooling, twitching her face, banging his head, smacking her lips, clicking his tongue, sucking on her hair, or picking his nose. When you ask your child why she does this, she will not know. She just seems to do this automatically.

Child-development experts at the Gesell Institute of Human Development say that these puzzling behaviors are not bad habits, but instead are "tensional" outlets. When your child feels stressed, he will do something to calm down. The more obvious behaviors are thumb- and finger-sucking, but many preschoolers do something else, such as sucking hair or head banging.

By age 5, most of these puzzling behaviors subside. Some parents choose to ride out these bizarre behaviors,

while others put boundaries on them and give their
a different, more acceptable tensional outlet. It all de-
pends on what you feel is best for your child.

Time Together

From time to time, all children act in puzzling ways. To
make sense of these behaviors, try some of these ideas:

1. When your child starts acting in a strange way,
help her identify what she is feeling. Ask questions such
as these: Are you feeling scared or are you feeling sad?
(Give preschoolers choices between feelings, since most
preschoolers won't be able to articulate what the feeling
is if you ask: What are you feeling?) Ask what you can
do: Do you want to sit in my lap, or do you want me to
rub your back?

2. Think about the ways you act when you're stressed.
Some people become more compulsive and have to have

SPOTLIGHT ON ASSETS

Asset 39: Sense of Purpose

When your child starts acting in puzzling ways, try
to pay extra attention to positive behaviors. For example, instead of speaking up when your child starts
chewing his nails, say something encouraging when
he behaves in a way that you prefer: "I really appreciate the way you've learned to sit quietly and look at
your books." When you celebrate milestones of mature
behavior, it helps your preschooler understand the
purpose of growing up.

---

all the bills in their wallet facing the same way. Some bite their nails or chew on their knuckles. Preschoolers aren't the only ones who act in odd ways when stressed. Get in touch with what you do so that you can be more empathetic when your child acts stressed.

3. Understand your child more by reading what's typical for your child's age. Three insightful books are: *Your Three-Year-Old: Friend or Enemy, Your Four-Year-Old: Wild and Wonderful,* and *Your Five-Year-Old: Sunny and Serene.* All three books are by Louise Bates Ames, Ph.D., and Frances L. Ilg, M.D. (New York: Dell Publishing).

4. Compare notes with other adults. Ask your parents about the unusual ways you acted as a young child. (You might be surprised!) Check in with other parents of preschoolers to find out how their children act when stressed. It often helps to talk about puzzling behaviors with others so you don't feel so alone.

5. If the behavior seems more severe and constant, you may decide to seek professional help. Consider how intense the behavior is, whether or not it has gotten worse, and how it interferes with other activities. Children who frequently bang their heads, rock their body from side to side, or obsessively suck their thumbs may have a more serious condition that needs a diagnosis and treatment plan.

Reading

What is the one skill that children need in order to succeed in school? Reading. The American Federation of Teachers cites research showing that a child who doesn't acquire reading basics early in life will have difficulty in every aspect of school.

That's why reading to your child and making reading a part of everyday life is so important. While your child will probably not be able to read independently until ele-

---

SPOTLIGHT ON ASSETS

Asset 25: Early Literacy

Choose books in which characters build Developmental Assets. For several creative ideas, check out *Playful Reading: Positive, Fun Ways to Build the Bond between Preschoolers, Books, and You* by Carolyn Munson-Benson (Minneapolis, MN: Search Institute, 2005). In addition to plenty of fun reading activities, this book also includes suggested books that focus on each of the 40 Developmental Assets.

mentary school, your child is learning *right now* about reading, even though you may not be able to see it.

The U.S. Department of Education recommends that parents read to their children for 30 minutes every day. Since preschoolers have short attention spans, divide these 30 minutes into small segments. Try reading to your child five minutes, and do this six times a day.

Take your child to your community or regional library. Get a library card in your child's name and let your child choose books to check out. Try to visit the library at least once a week, or as often as your time allows. Find out about story times and other events for preschoolers. The library is just as important to your child's development as the playground.

BONUS IDEA

Become Silly with Rhymes

Recognizing rhymes helps lay the foundation for reading and for getting ready for kindergarten. Make up silly rhymes that make your preschooler laugh, and soon your child will be doing the same. For example, "My cat named Matt sat on a rat. Boy, that cat was fat!"

Time Together

Reading is a fundamental skill that all children need to succeed. Even though preschoolers can't read, you can help pave the path to their reading (and more importantly, get them excited about books) by building essential skills, which experts call early literacy skills. Try a few of these ideas:

1. Surround your child with books. Collect sturdy board books and keep them with your child's toys so that she can pick them up whenever she wants. Encourage family members and friends to give your child picture books as gifts. Go to used book sales and purchase inexpensive books that get your preschooler excited. If your child attends a child-care center or preschool, ask if the center belongs to any book clubs where parents can purchase high-quality books for a small fee.

2. Make reading a part of your daily life. Read aloud to your child every day (and if you can, do it more than once a day). Integrate reading into your child's routine. Some parents read a book to their child before bed each night. Some even find waterproof books that can go in the bathtub. When reading aloud to your child, make the story dramatic. Use different voices for different characters. Occasionally act out (or ask your child to act out with you) a story that gets him excited.

3. Point out signs throughout your day. At the store, a lot of signs have the word "sale." See how many sale signs your preschooler can find while you shop. If you pick up a food can at the grocery store and read the label, talk about what you're reading. When you walk through the neighborhood, point out stop signs and other road signs. All these activities show preschoolers that symbols, letters, and words surround them.

4. Incorporate music and rhythm into your routine. Preschoolers often have an easier time remembering how groups of words go together when they sing them or clap them. Silly songs not only add levity to your child's day but also become favorites that your child wants to sing over and over.

5. Make reading a priority for yourself and all of the people in your family. Even if you don't have a lot of time, choose reading material that interests you—a daily newspaper, magazines, books, or a combination of any of these reading materials.

Rebellion

You want your child to do something, and your child refuses. Can you really have a 3-year-old rebel?

Yes. Although child-development experts don't use the term "rebellion" until the teenage years, any time your child resists doing something you want, you experience it as a form of rebellion.

SPOTLIGHT ON ASSETS

Asset 11: Family Boundaries

Keeping calm when your child disobeys will go a long way in teaching your child how to behave. If your child throws a tantrum, step away. Talk about the incident once she calms down. If your child refuses to pay attention, get down on her level and make eye contact. Waiting to talk respectfully sets clear boundaries about communication. After the incident has blown over, find ways to connect with your child and tell her how much you love her—even when you disagree.

For a child to separate and develop into a healthy individual, she needs to push away from her parents. Thus, every time your child resists, refuses, and says "no," she is forming a stronger sense of self.

The tricky part, however, is that you're usually not asking your child to do something outlandish. You want your child to eat healthy foods, get enough sleep, and cooperate with activities that help him grow. But there your child is: refusing to eat the broccoli, staying awake late into the night, and not picking up his toys.

What's a parent to do? Be aware of the power struggles and why they're happening. Begin to discern which battles are worth fighting and which require some creativity on your part. A preschooler who refuses to eat broccoli may eat it if you say that she can be excused from the table once she eats four bites.

Time Together

Throughout the preschool years, your child will resist doing certain things you want him to do. Your child will sometimes defy you outright. When your child refuses to cooperate, try one of these ideas:

1. React quickly when your preschooler misbehaves or disobeys. Be clear about what your child did wrong and what he could do to make it right. Children learn more quickly when the consequences are immediate and clear.

2. Consider responding in a way that will encourage your child to please you. Instead of getting mad about your child not combing his hair in the morning, say, "It makes me sad when you don't comb your hair like I asked."

3. Make your child's environment a safe one. Children are much less likely to get into trouble if you've eliminated

Give Your Child Choices

Whenever your child feels out of control (which happens when he misbehaves), give him two equally appealing choices of how to behave. This gives your child a sense of control and personal power and often will help him calm down. For example, if your pre-schooler refuses to wear the shirt you chose, give him a choice between two other shirts.

trouble from the room. For example, some adults spend a lot of time telling children not to play with or touch certain objects when it would be easier to remove those items and keep them out of reach.

4. Try to remember to spend a lot of one-on-one time with your child even when she is not misbehaving. Rebellious behavior can be a sign that she needs more attention in general. Let your child sit in your lap. Snuggle with your child when he wants to. Get down on the floor and play with your child. Self-assured children grow up to be more independent and have fewer problems.

5. If the misbehavior isn't too severe, ask before you scold. Your child will often tell you why she is acting in a certain way. Curiosity may have gotten your child into trouble, not outright defiance. Sometimes preschoolers will mimic the rebellious behavior of an older brother or sister. Or they'll swear because they overheard their uncle say an obscene word that made people laugh. When this happens, be clear about how you want your preschooler to act. If he objects because an older person is allowed to act in a way that the preschooler is not, say either that you disagree with the behavior or that people get more privileges as they grow older.

Safety

Accidents are the number one cause of death in preschoolers, which is why safety may be your number one concern as a parent. You need to supervise your preschooler at all times and keep your child safe.

Although preschoolers can avoid certain dangerous situations, don't assume that they can protect themselves. Because of the way a preschooler's brain develops, your child most likely will think only about her part in a situation—not anyone else's part. That's why preschoolers get hit by cars. A ball rolls into the street, and children think about only one thing: getting their ball.

As a parent, you may be surprised to learn that your child's safety often has more to do with what *you're* doing than what your *child* is doing. The American Academy of Pediatrics has found a number of factors associated with accidents in young children:

- A mother's pregnancy
- A change in the child's regular child-care provider
- Tension between parents
- A sick family member
- Moving

- The death of a family member
- Going on a vacation

Preschoolers will automatically be curious and get into things. Your job is to make sure that what your preschooler explores is safe. Monitor your child closely to ensure that you see any danger long before he does. When you are feeling especially stressed and distracted, reach out to other caring adults who can provide additional supervision.

SPOTLIGHT ON ASSETS

Asset 10: Safety

A key aspect of helping your child be safe is knowing the people around you. Get to know your neighbors, the caregivers your child has, and other adults around you. When adults know you and your child, they're more apt to keep an eye out for you. Not only does this keep you and your child safe, but it also builds a strong sense of community.

Time Together

Parenting a preschooler means being vigilant. You can do a number of things, however, to keep your child safe and be less stressed about it:

1. Always use a car seat for your child that is designed for your child's height and weight. Always place your child in the back seat. Read the car seat instructions carefully—car seats are not effective when they're improperly used. Even if you're on a tight budget, always invest in a new car seat, and be more frugal in other parts of your budget, such as your child's clothing and toys. A used car seat may have been involved in a car accident (which isn't always apparent), and some used car seats no longer meet current governmental safety requirements.

2. Closely monitoring and supervising your child at all times will prevent a lot of accidents. When you (or another adult) are watching your child, you can often see danger before your child discovers it.

3. Begin teaching your child simple rules about safety. Encourage your child never to pet any animal without asking an adult first and to seek the help of an adult when she feels afraid. This begins to help your child develop resistance skills which can be used in potentially dangerous situations.

4. Help your child become more comfortable with diversity (such as disabilities, different age groups, racial groups, and so on) so that your child can gradually learn

---

BONUS IDEA

Balance Risk and Opportunity

Children are more apt to grow up well when they feel relaxed (and are safe) than when they feel afraid. Your child does not need to know about a lot of the safety measures you're taking—or your anxiety about certain dangers. Keeping calm, creating a safe environment so that your child can act on his curiosity, and your constant supervision will go a long way in ensuring that your child grows up well—and safe.

to discern between danger and discomfort. (Adults who live in homogenous neighborhoods may also have trouble with this distinction.) Building cultural awareness and sensitivity shows your child that the diverse world is a stimulating, comfortable place to explore.

5. Visit your child's pediatrician or family physician on a regular basis so that you can keep your child healthy and safe. Pediatricians often have helpful information about childhood safety, and they keep up-to-date on new dangers and diseases.

Shyness

During preschool years some children are more apt to be shy. Researchers have found that shyness can often peak around the ages of 4 and 5 (and then return again during the early teenage years).

Some preschoolers are shy because they're wired that way. If so, you have probably noticed that your child was shy long before becoming a preschooler. Although all children go through separation anxiety between the ages of 8 and 12 months, some children have a tendency to be wary past one year of age. Their shyness kicks in when meeting new adults and children.

Separation anxiety and shyness are different. When children go through separation anxiety, they tend to cling to their parents and become wary of other people—even caregivers and favorite uncles. They may hide or cry when they're separated from their parents. Separation anxiety is a key aspect of developing a deeper attachment between child and parent.

Asset 37: Personal Power

Many shy children experience a faster heart beat and higher blood pressure because of the fear and stress they feel in social situations. To help your child, first emphasize how he can control what happens to him. Your child can go more slowly (when he feels ready) to meet someone new, and you can invite your child to sit on your lap or hold your hand when doing this. While helping your child feel more comfortable, teach other important social skills, such as making eye contact when you're talking to someone and learning to ask questions.

Shyness is a temperamental style. Shy children are slower to warm to new situations and new people. They need more time to adapt.

Don't worry about your child's shyness, and don't push her into social situations when she isn't ready. Instead, be patient and teach your child the essential social skills she needs. Even though she may be hesitant to meet new people, it's still important to learn these skills. Go slowly and work with your child on developing social skills.

Time Together

Many people have felt shy at some point in their lives. One survey found that two out of five adults experienced shyness when they were younger. Some people grow out of shyness, others don't. Either way, help your child with shyness by trying a few of these ideas:

1. Accept your child for who he is. Don't try to change your child and make him more bold and outgoing. (This can be more difficult if you happen to be outgoing and never experienced shyness yourself.) Your child will be more apt to grow up well with his shyness if you accept it as something normal.

2. Give your child time to warm up in social situations. Help your child feel secure and comfortable before doing something new or meeting someone new. When someone new appears, your child doesn't have to meet her or him right away. Once your child relaxes after someone new appears, try to create an interesting activity to lure your child into meeting this new person. For example, a toy or book often will capture your child's interest,

---

BONUS IDEA

See Shyness as a Strength

In our society, we tend to value outgoing people who make things happen. Yet, shy people also have a lot to contribute, and as long as they have strong social skills, they can grow up to be well-rounded, successful people. In fact, a number of famous people have struggled with shyness, including President Abraham Lincoln, astronaut Neil Armstrong, inventor Thomas Edison, mathematician Albert Einstein, United Nations leader Eleanor Roosevelt, and Clara Barton, founder of the Red Cross.

---

and her curiosity may become stronger than her sense
of shyness if a new acquaintance picks up the object.

3. Determine if your child is shy or introverted.
Some people get those two mixed up. Some children
are introverted. They prefer quiet activities, and they
often enjoy playing alone or with one child. Introverted
children aren't always shy; they just prefer to be alone.
So don't assume if your child doesn't embrace social situations that he is shy. A shy child feels anxiety in social
situations; an introverted child tends to seek quiet.

4. Become an advocate for your child. If the person
your child is meeting is more gregarious, pull the person
aside (if possible) and tell her or him that your child is
quiet in nature and needs time to warm up to new people. (A bold person often scares a shy child and will cause
a child to withdraw even more.) Avoid publicly labeling
your child as shy, since this may embarrass him or imply
that shyness is a weakness.

5. Find ways to help your child positively handle
her feelings and stresses. Some shy children need more
quiet time and space than other children. Help your
child become aware of her feelings, especially in social
situations.

Siblings

Parenting more than one child not only is more complicated because of the larger number of kids, but also because siblings fight and squabble. Not only do you need
to parent each child well, but you also need to help your
children develop a positive relationship with each other.

Because every child believes she should receive all your attention, you'll feel like a referee at times. Be firm about how siblings treat each other. Emphasize that every family member is important, that you love each one very much, and that you do not love one more than the other. As you teach these values, be ready to reaffirm them. Siblings will deal with these issues over and over as they grow.

SPOTLIGHT ON ASSETS

Asset 33: Interpersonal Skills

Help your children build positive relationships with each other by creating activities for them to do together, such as building a fort or finger painting. At mealtimes, have family members say one thing they like about each other. Everything you do to encourage your children to get along teaches them essential interpersonal skills they can use at home, at school, at the playground—everywhere they go.

Time Together

Siblings can have a delightful relationship—at times. Just like every relationship needs nurturing, so does the sibling relationship. The only difference with the sibling relationship is that both people are young and lack the needed skills to keep a relationship working well. Try these ideas to build a positive relationship between the siblings in your family:

1. Create big sister or big brother chores that only you and your eldest child do together. These activities help your older child feel close to you and give him unique tasks that a younger sibling isn't allowed to do. Also give your older child special privileges because of his age. This will help your child from acting too much like a baby or toddler.

2. Be on the lookout for hero worship, which typically starts around the age of 2. Younger siblings tend to adore their older siblings and love to follow them around. Monitor this closely since younger siblings tend to overstay their welcome while older siblings tend to dismiss and begin to resent a younger sibling. If you have an older child who is baby-sitting age, don't assume that she wants to baby-sit your younger child. It's often better to hire another teenager to baby-sit and let your older child baby-sit other people's children if she is interested.

BONUS IDEA

Let Your Child Stay Up a Bit Later

If you have more than one child, occasionally let one child stay up 15 to 30 minutes later than the others to get some of your individual attention. Some parents rotate this privilege among their children so that each child gets to stay up a bit later on a different night. Parents with partners can include their partner in the rotation to show children that adult relationships deserve extra time, too.

3. When you need to discipline one of your children, take the misbehaving child aside and do it privately. Otherwise, the child who is disciplined may be harassed by the others for being "bad" or "stupid." Be clear that everyone makes mistakes and can learn from their mistakes.

4. Know that you'll have more sibling rivalry if the age difference between your children is between 18 months and 3 years, says the American Academy of Pediatrics. Preschoolers (because of their age and development) also tend to be intensely jealous when a baby joins a family. You'll experience sibling rivalry, however, no matter how old your children are and how different their ages are. There will be days when you're convinced that your children hate each other. Be patient, and work on ways to develop the relationship between siblings by having positive family experiences together, such as movie night, game night, or walks together.

5. Create a weekly time to do something enjoyable together as a family. Go for a walk. Eat ice cream. Play games together. Foster a sense of fun between siblings.

Sleeping Issues

One of the best parts of parenting preschoolers is that they're much less resistant to going to bed—especially compared to toddlers. Many willingly head to bed in the evening, and most know that it's good to go to bed when they're tired.

What can be tricky is if you have a child who likes to wake up early in the morning (and most like to awaken long before their parents do), a child who wakes up in the middle of the night and wanders around your home, or a child who gets so involved in playing and other things that he resists going to bed.

Between the ages of 3 and 4, many preschoolers wake up in the middle of the night. Some get up and play for a little while. Some wander into another room and find something to do. Some even show up in your bed. Many parents are surprised to find their preschooler asleep in a different place (or room) than where the child started.

Although this is normal, it's helpful to put boundaries on this behavior. Decide if you're willing to welcome your child into your bed (but be forewarned that habits can be hard to break). Encourage your child to stay in her room rather than roaming around the house. Always ensure that outside doors are locked at night, with latches that small children cannot turn.

SPOTLIGHT ON ASSETS

Asset 23: Home-Program Connection

Although some sleeping issues are common and normal during the preschool years, others are not. If your child develops sleeping problems, talk with the program leaders of your child's preschool, child-care center, or program. You may be unaware of a stressful situation that is contributing to your child's sleeping trouble. (One big stressor for preschoolers is when a caregiver or program leader leaves and is replaced by someone new.) The more you know about your child's daily life, the more you can help her get the sleep she needs.

Give early risers a digital clock and tell them not to awaken you until a certain time. Tell them where they can play and what they can do so that when they awaken, they know the first place they can go. Preschoolers often enjoy having some solitary playtime in the morning, and they also delight in waking up a parent—when the time is right.

Time Together
Ideally you want your child to spend most of his sleeping time alone, but you can use a few strategies together to encourage him to sleep well through the night.

1. If your child wakes you up earlier than you'd like, suggest an activity or reward that your child could receive when she lets you sleep until the designated time.

2. Some children have a hard time staying in their rooms at night if they know other activity is happening in another part of your home. To counteract this tendency, some parents turn out the lights in the entire house for 10 minutes and create an overall quiet time for the household to signal that it's time for everyone to wind down. (You can always use a book light in another room to do a quiet activity until your child has settled down.) If your child starts crawling into your bed at night to sleep with you (and you don't want him to), take him back to his bed, rub his back, and then go back to your own bed.

3. If your child is afraid of the dark, plug in a nightlight. Remind your child that the light shines throughout the night and keeps watch over her.

4. Some children can keep going for hours (even late into the night) if they're doing something stimulating and interesting. If your child has a hard time falling asleep, create a routine that helps him quiet down. Sometimes, if you lie next to your child in the dark, he may fall asleep quickly.

5. Read a story together as part of your child's bedtime routine. Preschoolers love picture books. Check out seven each week from your library so that your child has a new one to look forward to each night before bed.

Social Gatherings

Throughout the year, your child will probably attend a variety of social gatherings: birthday parties, reunions, block parties, holiday events, family gatherings, and possibly a wedding or funeral. Since social gatherings each have different expectations and customs, you can help your child survive (and thrive) during a special event.

Asset 8: Children Seen as Resources

Social events go more smoothly (and are more enjoy-able) when children feel like valued members of an event. If you know other children will attend, consider planning activities for them to do together. Play a kickball game or a simple card game, such as Go Fish. Find simple ways to let young children contribute, like handing out spoons for ice cream or teaching a favorite song to the group. When children find a social event stimulating and fun, they'll be more likely to want to return.

Asset-building gatherings offer stimulating activities for children, but not all social gatherings are child-friendly. A number cater only to adults, and some (such as funerals and weddings) have an unspoken code of conduct for guests that may not be easy for a preschooler to follow.

At any social gathering, follow your child's signals by meeting your child's needs first. If the gathering is an all-day affair, you may need to find a quiet place for your child to take a nap. Bring along snacks, since some gatherings don't always have food available when your pre-schooler gets hungry, and also bring along some stimulating activities for your child to do.

If the special event is only for children, such as a child's birthday party, determine how long you should stay with your child. (If it's your child's first birthday party, you may want to stay the entire time.) Preschoolers can feel apprehensive (in addition to being excited) about a birthday party. You often can ease their distress by being present. Once your child is comfortable, give your contact information to the adults in charge and then leave. As your child grows and attends more social events, he will gradually learn how to act and how to have an enjoyable time.

Time Together

Prepare your child for a social gathering by explaining a few activities she may encounter. Answer any of your child's questions and let her bring along a comforting toy. Consider some of these ideas:

1. Don't assume that other people will interact with your child during a social gathering. Take your child around to the people you know and introduce them. Often your preschooler will talk with others if he sits on your lap or holds your hand. (For shy preschoolers, let them snuggle with you and warm up slowly.)

BONUS IDEA

Think Intergenerational

For reunions, block parties, and extended family gatherings, create a few activities that encourage people of different generations to mix and mingle. For example, create discussion starters, such as: What is your favorite food? What time do you get up in the morning? What do you do to relax? What do you think is funny? Have people partner up according to their birthday month or their favorite color.

---

2. If other adults and children are present, see if you can coordinate supervision between the parents. (Each parent can take a 15- to 30-minute supervision shift.) That way most parents will have time to visit with other guests, and the children will be supervised at all times.

3. Preschoolers enjoy children's birthday parties, but gift giving can be difficult for them. (Nearly every pre-schooler will want to open presents and keep them.) Some parents decide to buy two identical gifts: one for the birth-day child and one for their child to have *after* the party. Other parents ask their child to choose a favorite toy she already owns, then buy a duplicate as a gift. Learning to give takes some children a long time, so don't be alarmed if your preschooler is not an easy, cheerful gift giver.

4. Be clear that proper clothing and certain behaviors are important at formal events, weddings, and funerals. If your child resists, explain that everyone will be wear-ing the same type of clothes and that she can change clothes immediately after the event. Most likely your child will become curious when you dress up as well.

5. If you're planning a friend birthday party for your child, invite a small number of children (three to five) and have the party be short (about two hours). Many par-ents have preschool birthday parties during the lunch hour (from 11:00 A.M. to 1:00 P.M.) to ensure that they're not scheduling a party during nap time and to give pre-schoolers something they know how to do: eat a meal.

Stuttering

Many parents become alarmed when their preschooler—
who didn't have any trouble talking before—begins to
stutter and continues to stutter. The American Academy
of Pediatrics says 1 out of every 20 preschool children
stutter at some point, and that stuttering is more common
among boys. No one knows why stuttering becomes prev-
alent during the preschool years.

If your child begins to stutter, make note of it but
don't make a big deal of it. Listen to your child, but don't
correct your child's language. Usually stuttering will subside in less than two months.

Experts don't consider stuttering a problem unless
your child continues to trip over words for two or three
months—or longer. If that's the case with your child, visit
your pediatrician to see what you can do. Children with
severe stuttering may need to see a speech therapist.

SPOTLIGHT ON ASSETS

Asset 2: Positive Family Communication

Instead of correcting your child when he stutters,
continue the conversation as if no words were mis-
spoken. If your child stutters something about the
dog across the street, add details about the dog that
your child didn't mention. Making conversations an
enjoyable experience will help your child feel less flus-
tered and self-conscious about stuttering.

Time Together

Stress exacerbates stuttering, so do whatever you can to create a relaxed environment for your child. You can also help your child with any of these ideas:

1. Talk calmly with your child. If you become upset by your child's stuttering, calm yourself down so that your child doesn't pick up your anxiety (which will cause your child to stutter more). By speaking calmly and not overreacting, you model how to communicate in a relaxed, enjoyable way.

2. Focus on what your child does well. Ignore the stuttering if it rarely happens. Many times stuttering will disappear as mysteriously as it appeared.

3. If someone teases your child or makes a big deal of your child's stuttering, speak privately to that person. Encourage her or him to not tease your child. Explain that teasing makes stuttering worse—and your child more self-conscious.

BONUS IDEA

Simplify Your Language

Although using a large vocabulary helps preschoolers develop strong language skills, experts recommend simplifying your speech when your child stutters. Use simpler words and shorter sentences. Most preschoolers imitate the way adults talk, and simplifying your speech often helps ease your child's frustration. As your child stops stuttering, go back to your larger vocabulary.

---

4. Slow down. Preschoolers are often sensitive to the pace of family life. Some preschoolers may begin to stutter if life becomes too hectic.

5. If the stuttering persists and your pediatrician recommends a speech therapist, start the therapy as soon as possible. Many preschoolers with persistent stuttering overcome their speech difficulties by the time they enter kindergarten if the stuttering is dealt with early.

Swearing

It's shocking when your preschooler swears for the first time. Swearing tends to start around the age of 4 when children notice that swear words have a lot of power and can get a big reaction.

Swearing tends to appear around the same time your child begins to do other things that you disapprove of: lying, having intense emotional outbursts, and yelling that she hates you. It's a time when preschoolers are growing rapidly, testing the boundaries, and asserting themselves.

When preschoolers swear, most do not know the meaning of the words they're saying. They're using profanity for effect because they've noticed that swearing has power. They like to experiment with that power and see what happens next.

Try not to overreact when your child swears since the more attention you draw to his swearing, the more difficult it will be to get your child to stop. Calmly, yet firmly, say that swearing is not acceptable and then change the subject. Get your child chattering about something else, and often the swearing will subside.

Asset 22: Engagement in
Learning Experiences

Part of preschoolers' fascination with swearing is the sound (and effect) of words. Preschoolers are learning something important: words have power, and some words have more power than others. To teach your child the positive aspect of powerful words, help your child tap into her creativity and humor. For example, a child who says, "When I'm mad, I slurp salamander soup in the summer," will also get a reaction since she is saying something silly—and also thought-provoking. Playing with fun language helps preschoolers build vocabulary without getting into trouble.

Time Together

Although swearing is common among preschoolers, you do not need to sit idly by. Be clear about how you want your child to act—and speak. Try some of these ideas:

1. Be clear about which words aren't acceptable. What about the slang usage of certain swear words? Although some preschoolers stop swearing, they may call each other "toilet," "butt," or "poopy" as a way to elicit a response. Preschoolers often are fascinated by words that cause strong emotional reactions in other people.

2. When your child uses a swear word to express anger or distress, label the feeling and give your child an alternative way to express himself. For example, say,

"I'm mad as an angry lion. Rooaarr!" (Preschoolers love sound effects.)

3. If your child continues to swear even after you've been clear that it's unacceptable, search for the source of the swearing. Preschoolers do not make up these words, they pick them up from other people or the media. Once you find the source, talk with that person. (Note: If your child has an older sibling, that could be your source.) If the swearing is coming from a TV show, do not let your child watch that show.

4. What do you say when you're angry and stressed? Do you ever swear? Be intentional about modeling the kind of language you want your child to use.

5. Persistent swearing requires more of an explanation. Tell your preschooler that most people do not like swearing. They think the person is bad when bad words come out of the person's mouth. Some people lose friends because of swearing.

BONUS IDEA

Distract Your Child with a Good Book

Sometimes preschoolers swear because they get attention. Give your child some one-on-one attention by reading aloud a good picture book. If you can find a humorous book that plays with language, it may offer a selection of interesting new words that appeals to you both.

Thumb (and Finger) Sucking

Sucking a thumb is just as common among preschoolers as it is with infants and toddlers. Although some preschoolers no longer suck their thumbs or fingers, many still do.

For most preschoolers, sucking on a thumb or a finger helps to comfort them. If they feel uneasy about something, the thumb goes in their mouth and they often cling to something, such as a stuffed animal, toy, or even a blanket.

Child-development experts at the Gesell Institute on Human Development say that the time to help a child stop sucking a thumb or finger is between the ages of 5 and 6. That's when children are old enough to comply and find other ways to comfort themselves.

SPOTLIGHT ON ASSETS

Asset 40: Positive View of Personal Future

What matters most is how your child sees herself. Whenever your child feels relaxed, she usually is more open to trying different things. Having a positive outlook about new experiences is important to your child's identity. Whether you believe thumb sucking is right (or not) for your child, think about what's best for her. What helps your child feel less stressed in unfamiliar situations? What helps your child feel confident and optimistic?

Notice when your child tends to suck his thumb. Usually it's when he is tired, stressed, or unsure of a situation. Some suck their thumb at bedtime as a relaxing way to end the day and go to sleep.

A few children simply enjoy sucking their thumbs, and they're apt to do so much more than other preschoolers. (These are often the children who breast-fed well or the ones that pediatricians said "could teach others to suck" when they were only a few hours or days old.) These children have a strong suck reflex, and they find great comfort in sucking on a thumb, finger, or even their clothes and hair. Be patient with these children and know that they'll probably be slower in giving up their thumb sucking.

Time Together

Although thumb and finger sucking is normal for a lot of preschoolers, it's up to you to decide what you think is appropriate for your child. Try some of these ideas to deal with thumb and finger sucking:

1. When your child sucks her thumb, ask what your child is feeling. Help your child to articulate her feelings so that, over time, she sees that thumb sucking is related to feeling unsure or stressed. When your child can label her feelings, she will be more apt to let go of thumb sucking and seek other ways to comfort herself.

2. Any time your child experiences a major change (such as changing child care centers, going to kindergarten, moving, having parents get divorced, or having another child join the family), he will most likely suck his thumb more (or do some other type of comforting activity). Typically the thumb sucking will wane once your child feels less stressed and unsure of the change.

Monitor Other People's Reactions

Although you may not have trouble with your child's thumb or finger sucking, other people may. If another child teases your child, calmly say that everybody is different and your child is normal. Sometimes a child-care provider or another family member strongly believes that preschoolers should never suck their thumbs and gives your child a hard time about it. Talk with the person and encourage her or him to back down. If the person doesn't, you may need to switch child-care centers (since most likely this provider is being hard on your child for other reasons as well). Surround yourself with adults who respect your parenting.

3. If you want your older preschooler (around the age of 5) to quit sucking her thumb, create a progress chart to complete together. If your child can go one hour without sucking her thumb, place a star on the progress chart. Give rewards for accomplishments. Talk about how hard it is to change, and expect setbacks.

4. Talk with your dentist about the thumb or finger sucking during a dental visit. Thumb or finger sucking can push the teeth out of place. If your dentist recommends that your child stop sucking his thumb, ask your dentist to talk to your child. Then work together to help your child find another way to comfort himself.

5. Sometimes a preschooler will begin sucking a thumb or finger after giving up a pacifier. Usually these children have the strong suck reflex, and it takes them a lot longer to give up sucking.

Transitions

You know these times well: the times when you want your child to change gears, to do something different, or to change location. Your child most likely puts up a lot of resistance during these times. You're not the only one who has trouble with transitions. Many parents struggle with how to coax their child to move on to something else.

Since every day has many transitions (getting your child out of bed, getting your child to eat, getting your child out the door, getting your child to an appointment or program, picking up your child from a child-care center or program, getting your child into the bathtub, and getting your child to bed), it pays to learn how to

---

SPOTLIGHT ON ASSETS

Asset 8: Children Seen as Resources

Create a simple task that your child can complete while moving from one activity to another. For example, ask your child to carry a small item to the bus or car for you. If you're making a meal, ask your child to set a napkin next to each place setting.

---

help your child shift gears more smoothly. You won't feel so guilty about pushing her all the time, and she will become less stressed about these harried times. Plus, dealing with transitions and change is a major skill that children need to learn—and use—throughout their lives.

BONUS IDEA

Let Your Child Bring a Favorite Toy Along

Part of what jars preschoolers when they change location or move from activity to activity is that the change seems abrupt. Many preschoolers find it comforting if they have a favorite toy, doll, or stuffed animal that hangs out with them throughout the day. Then when your child needs to make a transition, so does the toy. After a while, you may overhear your child giving the toy, doll, or stuffed animal advice on how to make the change more smoothly.

Time Together

Being more intentional about making reasonable transitions can help to smooth them out. Try a few of these ideas to make transition times less stressful for both you and your child:

1. Build in extra time for transitions. Transitions are difficult when they have a short time frame. Leave a bit earlier so that the transition doesn't need to be rushed. If you're picking up your child from a child-care center or preschool, build in extra time so that your child can finish his activity. By spending a few minutes sitting with your child and doing the activity with him, you often can make the transition smoother for you both.

2. Be respectful of your child. Adults don't like to turn off the TV when they're in the middle of a TV show. Neither does your child. If your child is in the middle of an activity that has a set beginning and ending time, either change the transition time to coincide with the activity or figure out a way for your child to finish the activity later. (Some parents let their children watch only pre-recorded TV shows so that the show can easily be started again later.)

3. Focus on your child instead of the clock. During transition times, it's easy to get so caught up in the schedule (and being late) that your child can feel like a problem instead of a person. Your child will be less likely to dig in her heels when you take time to greet your child, look her in the eye, and ask how she is doing.

4. Create family routines that help with transitions. When children know what to expect, they're more likely to cooperate. For example, many preschoolers know that it's time to settle down when their parents read to them before bed. A routine reassures your child and helps make transitions smoother.

5. Give your child a time warning. Moving from one activity to another can feel abrupt. Give your child some minute markers to help. For example, say that it will be time to leave in five minutes. Then give one more warning around two minutes.

Traveling with a Preschooler

Although it may seem that a preschooler would travel better than an infant or a toddler, it often isn't true. Preschoolers become restless, and they can make quite a bit of noise about being restrained in a car seat—even for a short trip to the grocery store.

One key to traveling with a preschooler is to keep your child occupied so that he is focused more on an interesting activity than on the fact that he is stuck in a seat. The other key is to be firm about car seat rules. Your child must always sit buckled in one, no matter how short the ride is. Most car accidents happen under speeds of 25 miles per hour, and most happen close to home.

If you take your child flying, again insist on the car seat. Preschoolers are too old to sit in your lap to get the

---

SPOTLIGHT ON ASSETS

Asset 10: Safety

Make safety your number one goal in traveling with a preschooler. Require that everyone in the car ride in a car seat or wear a safety belt at all times. When your child gets restless, stop and take a break. Let your child run around a rest stop or a park for a short while. Never let your child get out of her car seat while traveling. If you do, you're giving your child the message that a car seat isn't always necessary. Be clear that everyone uses a safety belt, even when someone gets tired of wearing it.

advantage of flying free, but you may be able to get a child's fare, which can be about half the price of an adult. The Federal Aviation Administration strongly recommends that children sit in an FAA-approved car seat when flying. That means your car seat should include a label that reads, "This restraint certified for use in motor vehicles and aircraft." Some car seats fit only in cars because of their width. Those that are FAA-approved fit into a coach seat, which is about 16 inches wide.

Whether you're traveling to the bank or cross country, finding ways to keep preschoolers comfortable and stimulated will make the trip go smoother. Some preschoolers like to kick off their shoes or take off their coat while riding. Grant as many of their requests for comfort as possible and continue to keep them safe. Then give them something interesting to do so that the ride is worth taking.

Time Together

Traveling with a preschooler becomes easier when children have something to do. Some preschoolers actually enjoy traveling once they understand what to expect. Try some of these ideas to make your trip a smooth one:

1. Work hard to make the trip as comfortable as possible. You may want to give your child sunglasses or have a window shade for him. Use enough heat (or air conditioning) to regulate the temperature of the vehicle.

2. Be clear about traveling rules. Do not allow preschoolers to touch the door handles. (If your car has a child safety mechanism for the door, use it.) If you have more than one child, do not allow hitting, throwing, or yelling. If your children have difficulty riding together

Create a Travel Activity Bag

Let your child choose a favorite toy to travel with him, but also create a travel bag that has new, stimulating activities for your child. Consider bringing stickers, a large pad of blank paper, washable markers or crayons, a preschool activity book, and some other favorite toys. If you're taking a long trip, stop at your local library and check out picture books and books on tape to keep your child occupied. (Also bring plenty of snacks and something to drink.)

in the back seat, put another adult or older teenager between two children in the back.

3. If possible, see if you can find a toy car seat for your child's doll or stuffed animal to sit in. This helps teach her that everyone needs to ride safely. Your child also will become interested in keeping her doll or stuffed animal safe and will be insistent on always having that seat belt buckled as well.

4. Although you want a lot of activities for your child, make sure he isn't overcrowded. Your child should be able to reach activities easily and still have space to move his arms and feet.

5. If you're flying, check with the airline to see if it offers special items for kids. Some have a coloring book, a collector's airplane card, or a pilot's flying wings for your child to wear. When you board the plane, also ask the flight attendant if there are any special treats for children.

Violence

Everybody gets mad and wants to strike back at someone (or something) from time to time. So do preschoolers. The difference between a typical preschooler and a mature adult, however, is that preschoolers lack the self-control needed to express their anger appropriately. Thus, many preschoolers hit, kick, bite, throw things, and act in violent ways (much to the horror of their parents).

Although lashing out is a natural impulse for preschoolers, children need to learn not to act in these ways. They need monitoring so that adults can quickly intervene during aggressive acts and teach preschoolers to not act violently when they become upset.

SPOTLIGHT ON ASSETS

Asset 36: Peaceful Conflict Resolution

Children get mad, and children are going to act out when they're angry. Teach children how to resolve conflicts peacefully. If your child gets into a disagreement with another child, stay back and watch what happens. Some preschoolers can figure out for themselves how to negotiate a minor conflict, and you want to encourage your child to do this whenever possible. If, however, the conflict escalates and violence erupts (or you can see that violence is about to break out), intervene immediately. Give clear, simple messages of how to resolve conflicts peacefully: Calm down. Use your words. Say what you're feeling. Figure out what to do next.

Whenever your child becomes upset, teach her to use words instead of action. Help her to calm down and articulate her feelings. This sounds easy, but it will be hard. It will take your child a long time to learn this lesson since it's a human tendency to strike back. Continue to intervene immediately whenever your child acts aggressively, and give your child the same message over and over: Calm down. Use your words. Say what you're feeling. Figure out what to do next.

Gradually through the preschool years, your child will catch on and learn how to control herself when rage races through her body.

Time Together

Teach your child over and over how to act when he gets angry or upset. Try a few of these ideas to make your message clear:

1. Be calm yet firm whenever you break up a fight or stop your child from acting in a violent way. Remember that your child is watching how you act even when he is upset. The way you intervene and respond teaches your child a lot about how to act when feelings are strong.

2. Give your child a loving, stable home environment. This helps your child feel secure and comfortable, which will keep her from feeling agitated on a regular basis. Balance your loving environment with clear, simple rules so that preschoolers know how to behave. Violence— especially chronic violence—in the home will deeply affect a child and hinder her development.

3. Monitor closely what your child sees in the media. Keep your preschooler away from TV shows and movies that have violent themes. Make sure he watches only shows that are appropriate for his age. Limit the amount of media use so that your child spends most of his time doing activities that will help him grow and develop well.

4. Ask for professional help if needed. Some preschoolers act so aggressively that they can cause physical injury to themselves or others. If your child has a hard time learning not to act violently and continues to injure others, see your pediatrician immediately. A few

---

BONUS IDEA

Encourage Imaginary Play

To teach your child not to act aggressively, encourage your child to spend more time in imaginary play. Researchers from Concordia University in Montreal discovered that preschoolers who spent more time in imaginary play were more likely to negotiate peaceful resolutions for conflicts. Preschoolers who spend a lot of time in imaginary play also tend to talk more about feelings, such as "The monkey is sad" or "The horse is grumpy" or "The elephant is sick and doesn't like you talking to him." According to author Nina Howe, Ph.D., "Participating in make-believe play may give children a head start in mastering social skills." Tactile play materials, such as dough or finger paints, also can help your child process physical reactions in nonviolent ways.

---

preschoolers have conduct disorder, which is a serious condition that requires professional intervention. Preschoolers with conduct disorder who get professional help when they're young are much more likely to keep the disorder from growing worse (which leads to serious problems) and can find effective ways to learn how to control their aggressive impulses.

5. Teach your child the difference between accidental behavior and purposeful behavior. Most preschoolers assume that any conflict arises because someone wanted to be mean to them, when, in fact, a lot of fights break out by accident. Explain that everyone makes mistakes and accidents happen. The other child wasn't being mean, so revenge isn't necessary. Although this is a complicated topic to teach, it's helpful to begin emphasizing this early in your child's life so that she understands that most people are trying to do the right thing.

Other Resources from Search Institute

To learn more about Developmental Assets and how to use them with your preschooler, take a look at these resources available from Search Institute through its Web site at www.search-institute.org. Check out Search Institute's online catalog for even more videos, books, posters, and workbooks.

150 Ways to Show Kids You Care / Los Niños Importan: 150 Maneras de Demostrárselo. Even the simplest acts of kindness can build assets in the lives of children. This warm, inviting, and colorful book provides adults easy ideas and meaningful reminders about how they can show kids they really care. Based on the best-selling poster of the same name, *150 Ways to Show Kids You Care* is the perfect gift for parents, teachers, baby-sitters, youth workers, yourself, and anyone who touches the lives of kids, especially those ages 10 and younger. Includes an introduction to the Developmental Asset categories and 150 ideas in both English and Spanish.

Playful Reading: Positive, Fun Ways to Build the Bond between Preschoolers, Books, and You by Carolyn Munson-Benson. This book takes readers on a joyful romp through asset-rich children's picture books, emphasizing early literacy skills, reading for pleasure, and the eight asset categories. This collection is a terrific resource for parents, grandparents, teachers, child-care providers—anyone who spends time with preschoolers.

MVParents.com Created by Search Institute, this is an online resource for busy, caring parents who want information they can trust about raising responsible children and teens. Here you'll find easy, time-tested ideas and tools to guide kids in making smart choices and avoiding potential pitfalls. Parents can count on this Web site to cheer them on as they "stay in the game" and become the Most Valuable Parents they can be.

Raising Healthy Children Day by Day: 366 Readings for Parents, Teachers, and Caregivers by Jolene L. Roehlkepartain. This book of daily readings uses quotations, brief essays, and action statements to bring encouragement and inspiration to adults who care for children from birth to age 5. Each daily reading focuses on one of the 40 Developmental Assets, and by the end of the year, you'll have spent nine days on each of the 40 assets.

What Young Children Need to Succeed: Working Together to Build Assets from Birth to Age 11 by Jolene L. Roehlkepartain and Nancy Leffert. This book translates the 40 Developmental Assets into a wealth of practical, creative ideas for building all 40 assets for and with children from birth to age 11.

Your Family: Using Simple Wisdom in Raising Your Children. This compact booklet helps parents and caregivers with children from birth through age 10 reflect on their important role and the power they have to bring good things into the lives of their children. It introduces the concept of Developmental Assets, and it's a perfect tool for strengthening the positive qualities of families.

Acknowledgments

I appreciate the thoughtful work of Tenessa Gemelke, the editor of this book. It's an art form for an editor to be able to critique manuscripts at various stages and to inspire an author to make them even stronger. Tenessa does that, and I am grateful for that.

A number of other people have also been instrumental and helpful in my work with Search Institute's Developmental Assets for children. They include Nancy Leffert, Ph.D., of the Fielding Graduate University; Louise Bates Ames, Ph.D., cofounder of the Gesell Institute of Human Development; and Karen Vander Ven, Ph.D., of University of Pittsburgh's School of Education. Karen Vander Ven's extensive work on the 40 Developmental Assets for early childhood is impressive and has added breadth and depth to what parents need to know about parenting their young children well.

This asset-building movement wouldn't be anywhere, however, without the strategic, creative work of Peter Benson, Ph.D., the president of Search Institute. As always, I marvel at the daily contribution he makes in helping parents, other individuals, organizations, and communities better places for children and families.

Finally, none of this would be possible without my husband and parenting partner, Gene, and our two wonderful children, Micah and Linnea, who make family life more fun, much richer, and meaningful.

About the Author

Jolene L. Roehlkepartain is an author, parent educator, and national speaker on family and children's issues. She is the founder of Ideas Ink, a consulting company that focuses on the areas of parenting, children's issues, youth development, and education. She is the sole author of 25 books including *Fidget Busters, Raising Healthy Children Day by Day*, and *Building Assets Together.* She also is the co-author of 10 books including *What Young Children Need to Succeed.* She lives in Minneapolis, Minnesota, with her husband and her two children.

About Search Institute

Search Institute is an independent, nonprofit, nonsectarian organization whose mission is to provide leadership, knowledge, and resources to promote healthy children, youth and communities. The institute collaborates with others to promote long-term organizational and cultural change that supports its mission. Search Institute's vision is a world where all young people are valued and thrive. For a free information packet, call 800-888-7828.

Topical Index

Asset Index

Commitment to Learning
21. Motivation to mastery 9, 27, 132
22. Engagement in learning experiences 9, 27, 190
23. Home–program connection 9, 27, 181
24. Bonding to programs 9, 27, 96
25. Early literacy 9, 27, 165

Positive Values
26. Caring 10, 30, 87
27. Equality and social justice 10, 30
28. Integrity 10, 30, 120
29. Honesty 10, 30, 115, 144
30. Responsibility 10, 30, 147
31. Self-regulation 10, 30, 111

Social Competencies
32. Planning and decision making 10, 33, 84
33. Interpersonal skills 10, 33, 178
34. Cultural awareness and sensitivity 10, 33
35. Resistance skills 11, 33, 117
36. Peaceful conflict resolution 11, 33, 201

Positive Identity
37. Personal power 11, 37, 175
38. Self-esteem 11, 37, 150
39. Sense of purpose 11, 37, 65, 163
40. Positive view of personal future 11, 37, 192